W9-CHQ-014

DISCARD

THE NEHRUS

personal histories

THE NEHRUS
personal histories

MUSHIRUL HASAN

photo research, editing and captions
PRIYA KAPOOR

MERCURY BOOKS
LONDON

PHOTO CREDITS

Arun Nehru Private Collection:
14; 49; 60; 63; 112; 115 (top); 123; 141; 144; 145; 238; 239; 243; 289 (wedding card); 296; 297; 298; 299

Broadlands Archives Trust:
178 (top); 179

Corbis:
71; 181; 215; 190-191; 300-301

Fori Nehru Private Collection:
16-17; 17; 20-21; 39; 66; 106 (top); 142; 143; 272; 273

Getty Images:
174-175; 177 (top); 187; 194-195; 200-201; 202 (bottom); 287

The Hindu Images Archive:
139; 146; 147 (top); 148; 149; 152; 153; 156; 157; 158; 167; 170; 184 (left); 196; 207; 209; 212; 218; 220-221; 271 (top); 280; 281; 284; 290; 305; 308; 309; 312; 313; 314; 315; 316; 318; 319

Jawaharlal Nehru Memorial Museum and Library:
Cover; Back cover; 2; 6; 8; 10; 12; 18; 20; 32-33; 34; 36; 37; 38; 41; 42-43; 44; 45; 48; 50-51; 52; 53; 54; 56; 57; 64; 65; 67; 68-69; 70; 72-73; 74; 75; 76; 77; 78; 79; 80-81; 82; 100; 101; 102 (top left and bottom right); 103; 104; 105; 106 (bottom); 107; 108; 109; 110; 111; 113; 116-117; 118; 119; 120-121; 122; 124; 125; 126; 127; 128; 129; 130; 131; 132-133; 134; 135; 136; 137; 138; 140; 145 (bottom); 147 (bottom); 150-151; 154; 155; 159; 160; 161; 162; 163; 164; 165; 166-167; 168; 169; 171; 172; 173; 176; 177 (bottom); 178 (bottom); 180; 182; 183; 184 (right); 185; 186; 188-189; 190;192; 193; 194; 197;198; 199; 201; 203; 204-205; 205; 206; 208-209; 210; 211; 212-213; 214; 216-217; 217; 218-219; 222; 223; 224-225; 226; 240; 241; 242-243; 244; 245; 246; 247; 248; 249; 250; 250-251; 251 (letter); 252; 253; 254-255; 256; 257; 258; 259; 260; 261; 262; 263; 264; 265; 266-267; 268; 269; 270; 271 (bottom); 274; 275; 276-277; 278; 279; 282 ; 283; 285; 286; 288; 289; 290; 290-291; 292; 293; 294-295; 302; 303; 304; 306-307; 310-311; 317

The Masters of the Bench of the Inner Temple:
114; 115 (bottom)

Sarup Nehru Private Collection:
22; 23; 46-47; 102 (top right)

All copy work by Dheeraj Paul.

Preceding page 2: Jawaharlal after his release from Ahmadnagar Fort Prison, with Indira Gandhi, Feroze Gandhi and Rajiv Gandhi at Anand Bhawan, Allahabad, June 1945. Three generations of the Nehru-Gandhi family are seen in this picture—as are the three Prime Ministers the family gave India.

ACKNOWLEDGEMENTS

What began as a regular photo research project turned into one of the most enjoyable and fascinating assignments. As most Indians are so familiar with the subjects of the book, it was a challenge to find fresh and exciting pictures to make *The Nehrus: Personal Histories* into something more than yet another book on the Nehru-Gandhi family. Moreover the challenge lay not only in finding previously unpublished material but in being able to marry the very public face of the family with its personal side. We decided to overcome this by concentrating on the political and secular legacies of Motilal Nehru, Jawaharlal Nehru, Indira Gandhi and Rajiv Gandhi in the text, while allowing the pictures to narrate the personal histories of the family.

My search began at the Jawaharlal Nehru Memorial Museum & Library at Teen Murti House in New Delhi. The stacks of photo albums yielded some of the most beautiful, intimate and telling photographs of this extremely photogenic family. The camera loved them (especially Jawaharlal Nehru), but they loved the camera too! The Library also has private albums of close associates, and family members. This has made its collection one of the best in the country. Dr. Javed Alam of the Jawaharlal Nehru Memorial Fund was of great assistance in gaining access to both photographs and documents.

To go beyond the public sources we contacted various branches of the extended family. This led to meeting the three surviving grand old ladies of the Nehru family—Fori Nehru, Suraj Nehru and Sarup Nehru. These ladies not only provided us with photographs which only family members would have seen before, but also placed them in context by narrating anecdotes about family members and recollected stories of the strong family bond which used to exist between them. All three were extremely generous with their time and hospitality.

In Kasauli, Fori Nehru allowed us to go through her family albums and served us the best cheese toast I have ever tasted. Suraj Nehru, who lives with her son Arun's family, narrated stories of weddings, births and family reunions, all with a mischievous twinkle in her eyes. Arun Nehru and his family spent an entire day looking through old suitcases full of family albums— their search produced much success and some of the oldest pictures in *The Nehrus: Personal Histories* come from them. Sarup Nehru and her son, Nikhil Nehru, gave us all the material her husband, B.K. Nehru (junior), had collected in relation to the Nehru family tree. The family tree in this book is based on his hard work.

The gaps were filled by photographs from The Hindu Images Archive, one of the most organized and well-preserved collections in the country. Malini Parthasarthy very kindly gave us access to this collection and at their Chennai office T.S. Gopalan and K. Rajendrababu were of immense help.

At the Getty Images office in London, Charles Merullo, Liz Ihre and Ali Khoja were patient and indulgent of our many demands. Karen Robson, the Senior Archivist at University of Southampton Library, helped us gain permission from the Broadlands Archives Trust to use photographs of Jawaharlal Nehru at the Mountbatten's residence in New Delhi. Dr. Clare Rider of the Inner Temple Archives helped in gaining permission to use documents relating to Jawaharlal Nehru's time at Inner Temple.

The Nehrus: Personal Histories has been a charming experience for me as it allowed rare glimpses into personal moments of a very public family, a singular experience certainly worth sharing.

—Priya Kapoor

Motilal (standing extreme left) with friends and family aboard a *chikara* on the Dal Lake, Srinagar, Kashmir.

THE KASHMIRIS
cherished roots

page **15**

Motilal at the Coronation Durbar held in Delhi in 1911.

MOTILAL NEHRU
the patriarch

page 35

JAWAHARLAL NEHRU
destiny's child

page **83**

Rajiv Gandhi, Sonia Gandhi, Indira Gandhi (holding Rahul Gandhi and Priyanka Gandhi)
and Sanjay Gandhi, New Delhi, 1974.

THE NEHRUVIAN LEGACY

triumphs and tragedies

page **227**

THE KASHMIRIS
cherished roots

The continuing saga of the Nehru family, of the vicissitudes of Jawaharlal, Indira, Sanjay and Rajiv has been, for hundreds of millions of us, an obsession spanning more than three decades. We have poured ourselves into this story, inventing its characters, then ripping them up and re-inventing them. In our inexhaustible speculations lies one source of their power over us. We became addicted to these speculations, and they, unsurprisingly, took advantage of our addiction. Or: we dreamed them, so intensely that they came to life. And now, as the dream decays, we cannot quite bring ourselves to leave it, to awake.

—Salman Rushdie

In April-May 2004, India went to the polls. Political pundits predicted an outright victory for the ruling coalition. The people's verdict turned out to be different. Led by the Indian National Congress, the United Progressive Alliance performed surprisingly well. Sonia Gandhi, who was virulently attacked by the ruling combine politicians and their supporters in the media, struck gold for her party. But the greatest surprise of all came when she turned down the high office of prime minister and passed the baton on to the Cambridge-educated Dr. Manmohan Singh. This was an endearing but unusual gesture. 'Generations to come will marvel at Soniaji's renunciation of the seat

of power,' the Prime Minister acknowledged at the UPA government's first anniversary celebration on 23 May 2005, 'an act which is in the great traditions of sages and saints of this ancient land.'

Why this act of renunciation? The electorate was confused. The media had no answers. It is only the historian who knew that Sonia Gandhi had departed from not only an Indian tradition but also that of many of her family members who had long served the Mughals, the British, and the Indian Republic. 'I prefer the active virtues to the passive ones,' Jawaharlal Nehru had written in his *Autobiography*, 'and renunciation and sacrifice for their own sakes have little appeal to me.'

The Nehrus, Jawaharlal being the foremost among them, wrote their own histories. Their original name was 'Kaula', a word used in medieval Kashmiri texts for a devotee of Shakti, the goddess of power and energy. Their ancestors had undertaken the long trek from Brij Bihara, a small village in the Kashmir valley, to the Gangetic plain in search of greener pastures. Farukhsiyar, the Mughal emperor (1714-19), gave Pandit Raj Kaula, a Persian and Sanskrit scholar, the break. Raj Kaula moved to Shahjahanabad in 1716. Like all worldly men, he built a house along one of Delhi's canals (*nehr* in Farsi) and took Nehr-Kaul as his surname. Although the *jagirs* bequeathed to his grandsons—Mausa Ram and Sahib Ram—dwindled gradually into nominal rights, the family prospered. Pandit Lakshmi Narayan, Mausa Ram's son and Motilal Nehru's grandfather, served as the first *vakil* of the East India

A miniature painting depicting the Mughal emperor Farukhsiyar's court—Pandit Raj Kaula is seen seated in the first row, sixth from the right.

Above: Pandit Raj Kaula, Motilal's ancestor, was the first in the family to migrate from Kashmir at Farukhsiyar's request to join his court in Delhi around 1716.

Gangadhar, Motilal's father, was a *kotwal* (police constable) and held that position until his death at the age of thirty-four in 1861, six months before Motilal's birth.

Company at Delhi's Mughal court, a comfortable position for any new aspirant to the local bureaucracy. In 1857, his son Pandit Gangadhar, Motilal's father, was a police officer. In a little painting, he wears the Mughal court dress with a curved sword in his hand. His wife, Indrani, known as Jiyomaji, learnt Persian and quoted from its poets.

The Nehrus are Kashmiri Pandits. In the nineteenth century Kashmiri Pandits were concentrated in Lahore, followed by Lucknow and Allahabad, where the Ganga meets the Yamuna and the fabled subterranean stream Saraswati. Today, scores of Nehrus, Saprus, Tikkus, Katjus, and Takrus constitute a vibrant and enterprising global community. They set great store by education, projecting themselves as the bearers of learning, take pride in their love of literature, art and music, and draw comfort from their healthy attitude to life, their exquisite code of manners, and their delightful sense of fun.

Like all Kashmiri Pandits, the Nehrus have been conscious of their distinctiveness. One of them, Col. Haksar, recalled how he became aware of being different from other Indians: 'We were Kashmiris whereas everyone else was "they".' 'The Nehrus grew up guided by this unwritten code of behaviour,' wrote Vijaya Lakshmi, who was born

and bred in Allahabad. 'We were all one family living together in the manner of those days.' An illustration of the strong *biradari* solidarity is her description of the feast organized at their family home, Anand Bhawan (Abode of Happiness), on the occasion of her brother's marriage to Kamala Kaul on 8 February 1916:

In accordance with custom, after the return of the *barat*, the entire Kashmiri *biradari* (and nobody else) had to be invited to dinner. It did not matter whether the host knew the invitees or not or whether the guest was rich or poor, educated or uneducated, good or bad; he had obligatorily to be invited. Separate invitations were not sent out to individuals; the guest list, which only contained the names of the heads of families, was sent around to each of them, it being understood that the invitation was meant for all the members of the family, including children. The list was written in Urdu and the invitee would accept the invitation by writing the Arabic letter *swad* against his or her name. This is illustrative of the extent of Islamic influence on the Kashmiri community. One of the guests invited to these community feasts was a well-known drunk, Bishambar Nath Aga, who came presenting a pitiable sight, for his clothes were tattered and dirty, his face unshaven and he himself unwashed. He belonged to a very respectable family but had become so uncontrollable an alcoholic that there was no point in giving him any money or trying to help him in any other way. Nevertheless, such was the solidarity of the community that he was never excluded from any community function. All that happened was that he himself used to sit down at the far end of the *saf* (row).

This group identity, though fractured over time, still survives in large measure.

Were the Nehrus, then, aristocrats? 'No,' Ram Manohar Lohia, the Berlin-educated socialist leader and probably their most trenchant critic, said in Parliament. 'I can prove that the Prime Minister's grandfather was a *chaprasi* in the Mughal court.' Jawaharlal replied: 'I am glad the Hon'ble Member has at last accepted what I have been trying to tell him for so many years—that I am a man of the people!' That he was. At the same time, family traditions mattered to him a great deal. Thus Nicholas Nugent, Rajiv Gandhi's biographer, has shown how Jawaharlal, then in Allahabad's Naini Central Prison, had selected the name of Rajiv Ratna, his grandson, from lists that were sent to him, and how Rajiv inherited his name from both his maternal grandparents. The fact is that Jawaharlal very much wanted the family traditions to be preserved and perpetuated for the reasons that he mentioned to Indira Priyadarshini (as he called his daughter):

> To some extent you cannot get rid of the family tradition, for it will pursue you and, whether you want to or not, it will give you a certain public position which you have done nothing to deserve. This is unfortunate but you will have to put up with it. After all, it is not a bad thing to have a good family tradition. It helps looking up, it reminds us that we have to keep a torch burning and that we cannot cheapen ourselves or vulgarize ourselves…. If your grandfather's example strengthens and inspires you in any way, that is your good fortune. If your feelings towards your father or mother also help you in that way, well and good.

Some members of the Nehru clan had other ideas. Vijaya Lakshmi, known as Nan to her immediate family and friends, asked B.K. Nehru, India's future ambassador in the United States and High Commissioner in the United Kingdom, if the Nehrus had been a trifle arrogant. He agreed: 'And we have much to be arrogant about!'

Arrogance comes with success. And success, that is, 'white collar' employment in colonial India, depended on English-language education. The school or college was one gate to the society of the elite. Although not every member of the Nehru kin could afford or obtain such an education, quite a few did.

Like north India's Kayasthas or the Amils in Sind, two of the major groups that adapted themselves creatively to changing times, the Nehrus took advantage of the new opportunities for professional, administrative and clerical employment that had accompanied the expansion of British rule. Besides the pickings in government, a law degree offered the route to success and fame. This was because the setting up of law courts and an increase in litigation over land and debt had made the legal profession lucrative. In 1910–14, Kailash Nath Katju, a Kashmiri Pandit lawyer in Kanpur whose mentor was the same as Motilal's, that is, Prithvi Nath Chak, earned Rs 4,000–5,000 per month. Moreover, having acquired the status of

An early photograph of the extended Nehru family. Motilal, standing far right, is the only one in western clothes.

Below: 'The motherland sends you greetings.' A postcard from Motilal to his son Jawaharlal, dated 15 December 1905. Although the Nehrus had migrated from Kashmir in the eighteenth century, they retained their strong bonds with the Valley.

Evening on the Jhelum, Kashmir.

Motilal's sister-in-law, Nandrani (seated right), with her daughter Brajmohini and granddaughter Laxmi.

of seeing the Nehru name universally loved and respected is now being gradually realised. What single family in India can boast of such a galaxy of intellect among its scions as the Nehru family. B. Nehru M.A. (Oxon) of the Inner Temple Esq, Dr. K. Nehru M.B., Ch.B., B.Sc (Edin), J. Nehru M.A. (Cantab) of the Inner Temple Esq. And last comes the great scholar and scientist Dr. S.S. Nehru. Why, we should conquer the world with these and their descendants who I am sure will go on adding fresh lustre to the family name as the years go by.

Like the Kayasthas, the Nehrus were ready to navigate the crosscurrents of history with the aid of finer sensibilities that came with syncretism. This did not imply assimilation at the level of ritual or kinship or the dissolution of religious boundaries. It simply meant that one could be orthodox in one's religious beliefs but still contribute to the cultural intermixing that had become a norm rather than an exception in most parts of India. Indeed, prominent Kashmiri Pandit and Kayastha families could be highly rigid in observing caste restrictions, but they could still transcend caste and communitarian boundaries to foster cross-cultural exchanges.

Halide Edib, the Turkish author visiting India in 1935, complimented the Nehrus for overriding caste allegiance, a compliment from a remarkable woman whose secularity and revolutionary credentials acquired legendary proportions in Turkey and India. Yet another commendation came from Tej Bahadur Sapru, Allahabad's brilliant lawyer, who reminded Jawaharlal, 'Your whole education, your upbringing, and the makeup of your mind cannot permit you to think in terms of caste, creed, or colour.' The flattering remark came from a person who himself epitomized, both in his private and

airing and representing public opinion, lawyers began to exude confidence. Socially, membership in the profession enhanced their status and dignity.

Quite a few Nehrus joined the heaven-born—the Civil Service—and proved, by unremitting and detailed labour, their mettle beyond any doubt. Two of Motilal's nephews entered the ICS. Shridhar, son of Motilal's elder brother, Bansidhar, was one of them. Educated in Allahabad, Cambridge and Heidelberg, he joined the Civil Service in 1912 and held several key positions in the United Provinces' government (hereafter UP). His success offered the perfect occasion for celebration. Motilal, claiming to be the 'founder of the fortunes of the Nehru family', shared his joy with Bansidhar:

Shridhar's success is at last assured. What happiness—imagine Dr. S.S. Nehru B.A. BSc.(Alld.) double M.A. (Cantab) Ph.D. (Heidelberg) I.C.S. etc. My fondest hope

Kashmiris gained an advantage over others because of their knowledge of Persian that Zainul Abidin, the able and tolerant ruler, introduced in the Valley. This, along with their backgrounds and lifestyles, also allowed them to be a bridge between elite Hindus and Muslims. (Nandlal is seen standing in the back, extreme left.)

public persona, the inclusive character of north India's composite culture.

The collapse of the Mughal empire had spurred important changes. Winds of change and reform swept the towns and the countryside. New ideas flowed; new structures replaced old ones. Yet the social and cultural equilibrium among castes and communities remained unchanged, as also the norms guiding interpersonal relationships and cross-community networks. Religious zealots contested this pluralist inheritance in order to popularize their own version of Islam and Hinduism, but this legacy, a capital accumulated over centuries, continued to devolve downwards to become part of everyday culture. In Yahiyapur, a locality in Allahabad, Hindus venerated the shrines of Muslim saints and a Hindu pleader took out a *tazia* during Muharram in the 1880s. Even after the turn of the century, Hindus voted for Muslim candidates in municipal elections and vice versa. In most other parts of UP, too, Hindu and Muslim culture remained inextricably and happily entwined.

Jawaharlal talked of growing up in north India, with its 'mixture of what is sometimes called Muslim culture in language, in ways of life, and food etc.' 'So,' he added, 'I became used to this composite kind of cultural life.' His niece, Nayantara Sahgal, saw it all: a tradition of serene and symmetrical architecture, an elegant school of dance, Hindi and Urdu prose and poetry, and excellent cuisine. In July 1940, Sapru reminded the young Kashmir Pandits in Srinagar that their forefathers and compatriots in other parts of India owed a great deal to a joint culture:

> Who does not know that in northern India, at any rate, it was the Kashmiri Pandit who summed up in himself the best that there was to be found both in Hindu and Muslim cultures? It was his proficiency in Persian that secured for him a distinct position in the bureaucracy of the Mughal times, and, I say this with confidence when I remember the history of those of our ancestors who were compelled by circumstances to migrate from Kashmir and to seek their fortune in what is now British India. They carried with them their keen intellect, their remarkable sense of adaptability and their character into a larger and competitive world, and so long as Persian was the official language at the Courts of Delhi and Lucknow, the Kashmiri Pandit shared with the Kayastha some of the highest offices in Mughal Times. But it is not merely as an official that the Kashmiri Pandit figured in Lahore, Delhi and Lucknow. His position as a man of culture and letters was distinct and was acknowledged by Muslim rulers. When Persian was ousted by Urdu, it did not take the Kashmiri Pandit much time to make his mark on the altered situation.

THE NEHRU FAMILY TREE

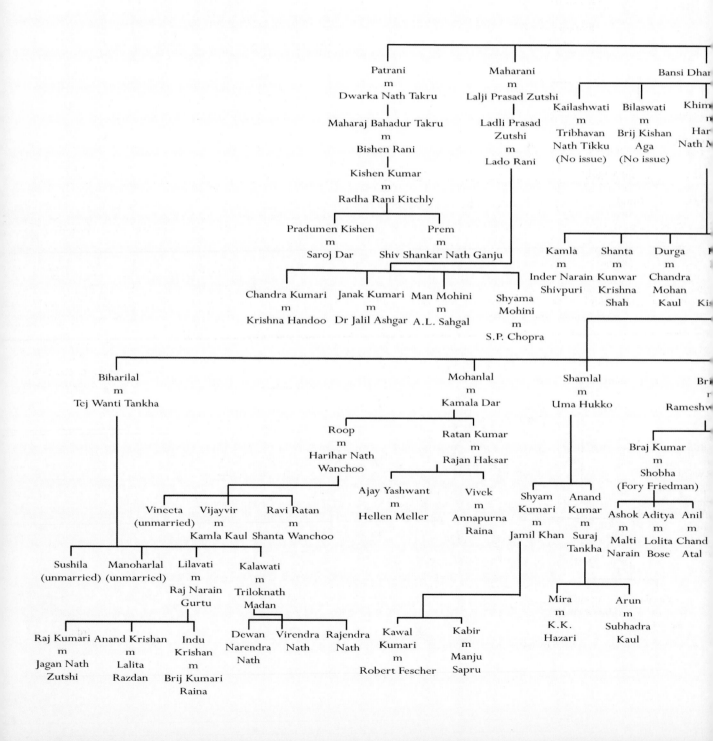

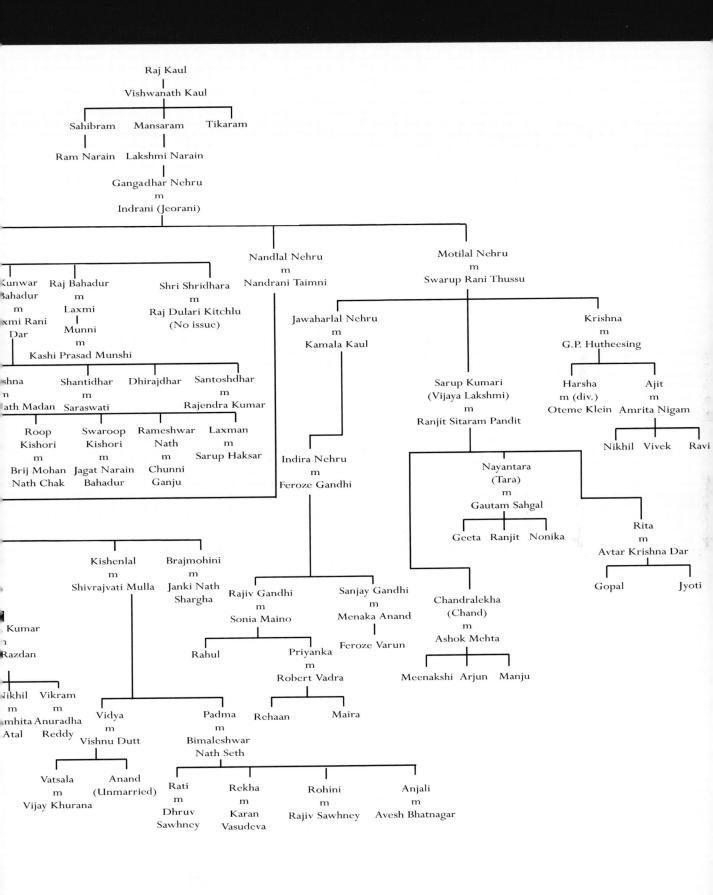

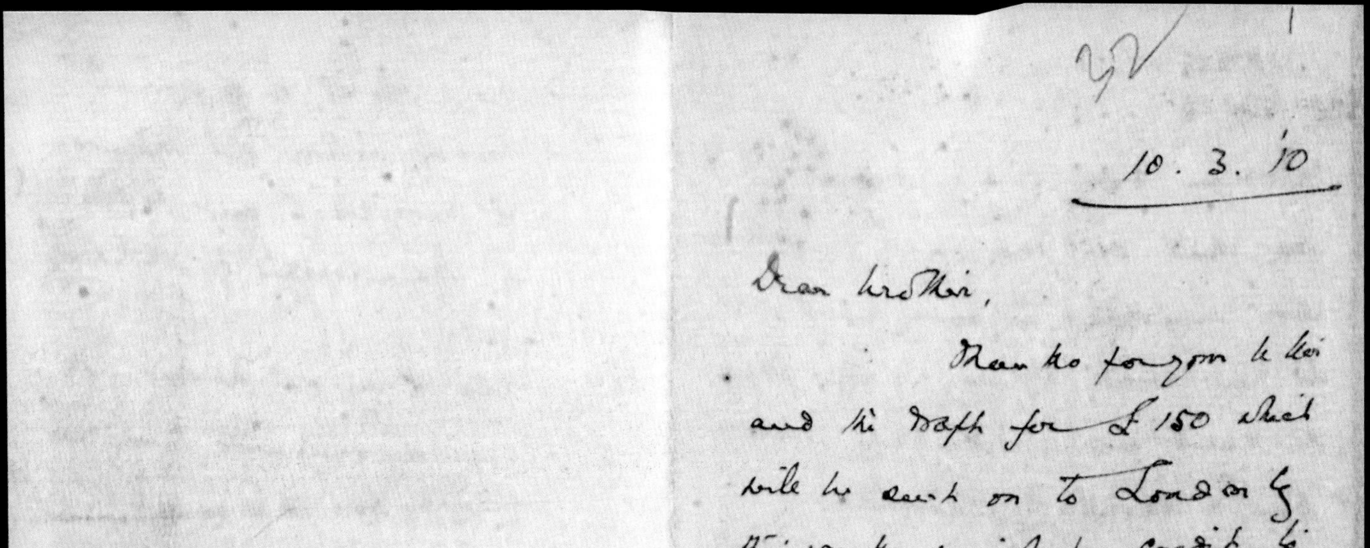

10.3.10

Dear brother,

Thanks for your letter and the draft for £150 which will be sent on to London by this week's mail for credit to Stri Dhar's account.

The Government have asked for a short family history of mine. I know nothing about it. Will you kindly send me a note on the subject? Is there any mention of any of our ancestors in any published book or report?

12

Motilal wrote to his brother Bansidhar on 10 March 1910 asking him for details of the Nehru family history.

Diwan Narendra nath once told me that our maternal grandfather was mentioned in some book that he had seen – I have no idea what the book was. I think the following points should be brought out in your note :

1. The date & circumstances of our migration from Kashmir

2. Any important public office held by any of our ancestors since the migration.

3. Did any of our ancestors held landed property or Jagir

4. Short sketch of the general family history with references if possible to any publications or manuscripts of authority.

I do hope I am not putting you to greater inconvenience than you can bear. But it is impossible for me to do so without your assistance.

Yours affly

Motilal Nehru

CHRONOLOGY

1861 Motilal, son of Gangadhar, born in Agra on 6 May.

1888 Motilal attends the Allahabad Congress session as a delegate.

1889 Motilal elected to the subjects committee at the Bombay Congress session.

Jawaharlal born on 14 November in Allahabad.

1892 Motilal appointed secretary of the reception committee at the Allahabad Congress session.

1900 Motilal and Swarup Rani's first daughter Sarup Kumari is born on 18 August.

1907 First provincial conference of the United Provinces opens in Allahabad with Motilal in the chair.

Motilal and Swarup Rani's second daughter Krishna Kumari is born in November.

1910 Motilal successfully contests in the enlarged provincial council under the 'reformed' constitution as per the Minto-Morley Reforms.

Elected vice chairman of the reception committee at the 26th Congress session held at Allahabad.

1911 Motilal, his wife and daughters attend the Coronation Durbar in Delhi.

1912 Jawaharlal returns to India and joins the Allahabad High Court as a lawyer.

Motilal and Jawaharlal attend the Congress session at Bankipur.

1915 Jawaharlal speaks for the first time from a political platform.

1916 Jawaharlal marries Kamala Kaul in Delhi on 8 February.

Jawaharlal attends the Lucknow Congress session and meets M.K. Gandhi.

1917 Motilal and Jawaharlal join the Home Rule League.

Indira Priyadarshini, daughter of Jawaharlal and Kamala, is born on 19 November in Allahabad.

Motilal meets Edwin S. Montagu, Secretary of State for India, in Delhi.

Motilal drifts away from the 'moderates' in the Congress party on the basis of the Montagu-Chelmsford Report.

1918 Motilal speaks at the plenary session of the Congress in Bombay.

Jawaharlal becomes secretary of the Home Rule League.

1919 The Jallianwala Bagh massacre takes place on 13 April.

Motilal appointed to the Congress sub-committee to collect and produce evidence before the Hunter Committee on the Jallianwala Bagh massacre.

Motilal starts a newspaper, *The Independent*.

1920 Motilal elected as President of the Amritsar Congress session.

Nehru family joins the non-cooperation movement.

1921 Motilal resigns from the legislative assembly and stops his legal practice.

Motilal and Jawaharlal are arrested for the first time.

Motilal elected member of the Congress Working Committee and one of the three general secretaries.

Sarup Kumari marries Ranjit Pandit on 10 May.

1922 Motilal, C.R. Das and Hakim Ajmal Khan found the Swaraj Party on the issue of entry into the Viceroy's Council.

1923 Motilal leads the Swaraj Party in the Central Legislative Assembly.

Jawaharlal elected chairman of the Allahabad Municipal Board in April.

Jawaharlal arrested on 19 December for defying an order banning entry into Nabha state.

Jawaharlal becomes general secretary of the Congress from 1923-25.

1924 Motilal's maiden speech in the legislature.

Swarajist given the majority seats in the governing committee.

1925 Rift within the Swaraj Party between Motilal and those arguing for 'responsive co-operation' with the British.

1926 Motilal and Maulana Azad issue manifesto of 'The Indian National Union'.

Jawaharlal visits Europe for Kamala Nehru's treatment.

1927 Jawaharlal attends the Congress of Oppressed Nationalities in Brussels in February.

Jawaharlal moves the 'Independence Resolution' at the Madras Congress session.

Jawaharlal becomes general secretary of the Congress party till 1929.

1928 Motilal presides over the sub-committee to determine the principles of an Indian Constitution.

Motilal presides over the Calcutta Congress session.

Indira starts the children's section of Gandhi's Charkha Sangh.

1929 Jawaharlal presides over the Nagpur session of the All India Trade Union Congress in November.

Jawaharlal presides over the Lahore Congress session.

1930 Motilal and Jawaharlal arrested for participating in the Salt Satyagraha.

Indira organizes the Allahabad branch of the Vanar Sena.

Motilal released on health grounds in September.

Motilal declares 16 November as 'Jawahar Day' to protest against the two-and-a-half-year sentence passed on Jawaharlal.

1931 Motilal passes away on 6 February.

Jawaharlal jailed again.

1933 Krishna Kumari marries Raja Hutheesing on 20 October.

1934 Jawaharlal organizes relief for the victims of the Bihar earthquake.

Jawaharlal arrested for making anti-government speeches.

1936 Kamala Nehru passes away on 28 February in Lausanne, Switzerland.

Jawaharlal presides over the Lucknow Congress session.

Jawaharlal travels all over the country campaigning for the Congress party for the general elections.

Jawaharlal presides over the Faizpur Congress session.

1938 Jawaharlal selected chairman of the National Planning Committee.

Swarup Rani passes away on 10 January.

1939 Jawaharlal drafts the Congress resolution on the Second World War.

1940 Jawaharlal chosen to be the second satyagrahi in the Individual Satyagraha Movement.

Jawaharlal arrested on 31 October for speeches he made in Gorakhpur.

1942 Indira marries Feroze Gandhi in Allahabad on 26 March.

Jawaharlal negotiates with Sir Stafford Cripps and on 7 August moves the Quit India Resolution at a Congress meeting.

Jawaharlal arrested on 9 August.

Indira Gandhi and Feroze Gandhi attend the Bombay Congress session.

Indira Gandhi addresses a meeting at Allahabad and is subsequently arrested on 11 September.

1944 Indira Gandhi and Feroze Gandhi's first child Rajiv Ratna is born on 20 August.

1945 Jawaharlal released from jail on 15 June.

Jawaharlal represents the Congress at the Simla Conference.

Jawaharlal represents the Indian National Army officers as their lawyer.

Jawaharlal elected as president of the All-India States Peoples Conference in December.

1946 Indira Gandhi and Feroze Gandhi's second son Sanjay is born on 14 December.

Jawaharlal holds talks with members of the British Cabinet Mission.

Jawaharlal elected Congress President in May (resigned in September).

Interim government formed on 2 September with Jawaharlal as vice president of the Viceroy's Executive Council and member of External Affairs and Commonwealth Relations ministries.

On 13 December Jawaharlal moves the 'Objectives Resolution' in the Constituent Assembly.

1947 Jawaharlal addresses the nation accepting the British government's plan for the transfer of power to India.

Moves the resolution on the 'National Flag' in the Constituent Assembly on 22 July.

Jawaharlal becomes the first Prime Minister of India on 15 August.

He holds the External Affairs and Commonwealth Relations portfolios also.

1948 Jawaharlal attends the Commonwealth Prime Ministers' Conference in London in October.

Jawaharlal addresses the United Nations General Assembly in Paris on 3 November. Indira Gandhi accompanies her father to Europe.

1949 On 20 January Jawaharlal inaugurates a conference of 18 nations to condemn Dutch aggression against Indonesia.

Visits USA and Canada for the first time.

1950 India becomes a Republic on 26 January.

Jawaharlal becomes chairman of the Planning Commission in March (holds this position until his death in 1964).

1951 Jawaharlal elected President of the Congress (continues until 1954).

1952 Jawaharlal forms a new government after the first General Elections.

Inaugurates the first Community Development Project in October.

1953 Chief Ministers' conference held in New Delhi in November.

1954 Jawaharlal holds talks with Chinese Premier Chou En-Lai in June. Issues a joint statement on 28 June outlining the five principles (Panchsheel) for the regulation of relations between nations.

1955 Jawaharlal moves the 'Socialistic Pattern of Society' resolution at the Awadhi session of the Congress.

Jawaharlal attends the Asian-African Conference held in Bandung from 18-24 April.

Indira Gandhi appointed as member of the Central Election Committee of the Congress and is elected President of the Allahabad City Congress.

1956 Jawaharlal meets President Nasser of Egypt and President Tito of Yugoslavia at Brinoi, 18-19 July. They discuss coexistence and the need for disarmament.

Jawaharlal attends the Colombo's Power conference in New Delhi from 12-14 November to discuss the international session with special reference to the Anglo-French-Israeli aggression against Egypt, and Soviet intervention in Hungary.

1957 Jawaharlal forms a new government in April after the second General Elections.

1958 Indira Gandhi appointed member of the Central Parliamentary Board in place of Jawaharlal.

1959 Jawaharlal sponsors a resolution on co-operative farming and state trading of food grains at the Nagpur Congress session.

1960 Jawaharlal and Chou En-Lai hold talks in April for easing the Sino-Indian border tension.

Jawaharlal visits Pakistan to sign the Indus Water Treaty.

Jawaharlal addresses the UN General Assembly in New York on 3 October.

Feroze Gandhi passes away on 8 September.

Indira Gandhi elected member of UNESCO Executive Board.

1961 Jawaharlal attends the Conference of Non Aligned Nations in Belgrade in September.

1962 Jawaharlal forms a new government after the third General Elections.

Jawaharlal presides over the National Integration Council meeting in June.

China attacks India on 20 October and the two countries fight a one-month border war.

1963 'Kamraj Plan' initiated - under which ministers relinquish office to reorganize the Congress Party.

Indira Gandhi elected chairperson of Central Citizens' Committee.

1964 Jawaharlal falls ill during the 68th session of the Congress party, held in Bhubaneswar in January.

Jawaharlal passes away on 27 May at his home, Teen Murti House, New Delhi.

Indira Gandhi appointed Minister of Information & Broadcasting in Lal Bahadur Shastri's cabinet.

Indira Gandhi elected unopposed to Rajya Sabha.

1965 The second Indo-Pak war takes place.

1966 Indira Gandhi elected leader of the Congress Party in Parliament following Shastri's death in Tashkent.

Indira Gandhi sworn in as India's third Prime Minister on 24 January.

Indira Gandhi holds tripartite meeting with Presidents Tito and Nasser in Delhi.

1967 Fourth General Elections held.

Indira Gandhi elected to the Lok Sabha from Rae Bareli and unanimously elected leader of the Congress Parliamentary Party.

Indira Gandhi sworn in as the Prime Minister on 13 March.

Krishna Hutheesing passes away.

1968 Rajiv Gandhi marries Sonia Maino on 25 February in New Delhi.

1969 Debate and nomination for Presidential election creates rift at the Congress session held in Bangalore.

Indira Gandhi takes over Finance portfolio from Morarji Desai. 14 major banks are nationalized on 19 July and privy purse is abolished.

Indira Gandhi is expelled from the 'Congress party' on 12 November.

Indira Gandhi donates Anand Bhawan to the nation.

1970 Indira Gandhi attends the Third Conference on Non-Aligned countries at Lusaka.

Addresses the silver jubilee session of the UN in New York.

Parliament dissolved on Indira Gandhi's advice and fresh elections announced.

Rajiv Gandhi and Sonia Gandhi's first child, Rahul, is born on 19 June.

1971 Absolute majority for Congress in the General Elections.

Indira Gandhi re-elected as leader of the Congress Parliamentary Party.

Indira Gandhi is sworn in as Prime Minister on 18 March.

Rajiv Gandhi and Sonia Gandhi 's daughter, Priyanka, is born on 11 January.

In December India takes defensive action after being attacked by Pakistan and recognition of Bangladesh is announced in the Lok Sabha soon after.

1972 Indo-Pak agreement signed at Simla between Indira Gandhi and Zulfiqar Ali Bhutto in July—marking the formal end of the Bangladesh war.

Indira Gandhi receives the Bharat Ratna on 26 January.

1973 Delhi Agreement signed on Indo-Bangladesh-Pakistan humanitarian issues and return of prisoners of war on 28 August.

Indira Gandhi attends the fourth Conference of Non-Aligned Countries in Algeria.

1974 India becomes the world's sixth nuclear power when it explodes a nuclear device in the Rajasthan desert.

Sanjay Gandhi marries Maneka Anand on 29 September in New Delhi.

1975 Indira Gandhi declares Emergency on 25 June—two weeks after the Allahabad High Court finds her guilty of corrupt electoral practices.

1976 Under the 42nd amendment to the Constitution, India becomes a 'socialist secular' nation.

1977 After the sixth General Elections Indira Gandhi resigns as Prime Minister on 22 March.

Janata Party comes to power.

1978 Parliament sentences Indira Gandhi to prison on 19 December, until the end of the session (a period of one week), for obstructing an enquiry into the Maruti car project.

1980 Indira Gandhi is sworn in as Prime Minister again on 14 January after Congress triumphs in the seventh General Elections.

Sanjay and Maneka Gandhi's son, Feroze Varun, is born on 13 March.

Sanjay Gandhi is killed in a flying accident on 23 June in New Delhi.

1981 Rajiv Gandhi successfully contests the Amethi by-elections on June 15.

1982 The IX Asiad Games are held in New Delhi under the supervision of Rajiv Gandhi.

1983 Rajiv Gandhi is appointed secretary general of the Congress on 2 February.

1984 Indira Gandhi sends the army into the Golden Temple in Amritsar to flush out Sikh extremists.

Indira Gandhi is assassinated by her own bodyguards in New Delhi on 31 October .

Rajiv Gandhi is sworn in as Prime Minister the same evening.

Rajiv Gandhi leads the Congress to a landslide victory in the General Elections and is sworn in as Prime Minister again on 31 December 1984.

1985 Rajiv Gandhi visits USSR for the first time in May.

Rajiv Gandhi inaugurates the Festival of India in France and USA later that year.

Rajiv Gandhi addresses the UN for the first time on 24 October.

Rajiv Gandhi formally inaugurates the Congress centenary celebrations on 27 December.

1986 The controversial decision taken by the ruling Congress party under the leadership of Rajiv Gandhi in the Shah Bano case spurs a debate on a universal civil code in India.

Rajiv Gandhi escapes an assassination attempt, at Rajghat, Delhi.

The second SAARC summit is held in Bangalore in November.

1987 Rajiv Gandhi sends Indian peacekeeping forces to Sri Lanka to end Tamil-Sinhalese violence.

Rajiv Gandhi escapes an attempt on his life by a Sri Lankan naval guard in Colombo.

In October Rajiv Gandhi visits the Commonwealth Heads of Government Meeting in Vancouver.

1989 Falling public support leads to Congress defeat in general elections. Rajiv Gandhi steps down as Prime Minister.

Minority government, led by V.P. Singh, comes to power.

1990 Indian troops withdrawn from Sri Lanka.

Vijaya Lakshmi Pandit passes away.

1991 General elections are announced after the fall of the V.P. Singh government.

Rajiv Gandhi is assassinated on 21 May by a LTTE suicide bomber in Sriperumbudur, Tamil Nadu.

Congress leader P.V. Narasimha Rao sworn in as the Prime Minister on 21 June.

Economic reform programme begun by the Prime Minister.

1992 Kar sevaks demolish the 450-year-old Babri Masjid in Ayodhya on 6 December.

1996 Eleventh General Elections held in May.

Congress suffers worst ever electoral defeat as the BJP as the largest single party.

1997 Priyanka Gandhi marries Robert Vadra on 18 February in Delhi.

1998 India carries out nuclear tests under the BJP government.

Sonia Gandhi enters politics.

Sonia Gandhi becomes the fifth member of her family to take over as Congress President in March.

1999 Sonia Gandhi elected to Parliament.

Sonia Gandhi offers to resign as Congress President after leaders challenge her right as someone not born of Indian soil to try to become India's Prime Minister.

2004 The Delhi High Court ruled on 4 February that 'Sixteen years of investigation by a premier agency of this country (the CBI) could not unearth a scintilla of evidence against (Rajiv Gandhi and S.K. Bhatnagar) for having accepted bribe/illegal gratification in awarding the contract' to Bofors.

Maneka Gandhi and Feroze Varun Gandhi join the BJP in February.

Announcement of early national elections for the fourteenth Lok Sabha from 20 April to 10 May.

The General Elections end on 10 May, leading to the decisive defeat of the National Democratic Alliance.

Rahul Gandhi elected to Parliament from Amethi.

Sonia Gandhi announces her decision to 'humbly decline this post' (Prime Minister) on 18 May.

Dr. Manmohan Singh appointed Prime Minister by President Abdul Kalam on 19 May.

There is no record of the history of the family, all the old papers & documents being destroyed in the mutiny of 1857. The oldest living member of the family is my brother Pandit Bansi Dhar Nehru, a Govt. pensioner, who retired from the post of Subordinate Judge of the 1st Grade in these Provinces some 13 years ago and is now 68 years old. He has furnished the following account ~~that is~~ the early part of which is mainly based on family tradition.

In the maternal line my great grand father was the Diwan of Shamru ki Begum (the Begum of Dyce Sombres.) My grand father Pandit Shanker nath Zutshi was a famous man of letters at Dilli and is mentioned by the late Sir Syed Ahmad Khan in his book entitled A'sár-us-Sanadid at p. 122.

I am the youngest of three brothers - The Eldest Pandit Bansi Dhar Nehru already mentioned is now living in retirement at Mathra (U.P.) The next was Pandit Nandlal Nehru who served as Diwan in the Khetri State (Rajputana) with great credit for some ten years and in that capacity rendered signal services to the Thaggi & Dacoiti Department of the British Government ~~for~~ which he received several Kharitas and letters in recognition of his services

On the death of the then Raja he removed to Allahabad and having qualified as a Vakil of the High Court soon made his way to the front ranks of the profession He died suddenly in the prime of life in 1887.

I was born at Agra on the 6th May 1861 and was Educated at the Govt. Schools at Allahabad and Cawnpore and the Muir Central College. I was enrolled as a Vakil of the High Court in 1883 and in January 1896 was admitted to the roll of Advocates by unanimous resolution of the Chief Justice and the Hon'ble Judges then constituting the Court. In Aug 1909 I was permitted to appear and plead at the bar of the Judicial Committee of the Majesty's Privy Council. In Dec. 1909 I was elected a member of the Legislative Council of His Honor the Lieutenant Governor of the United Provinces by the delegates of the Allahabad Division.

3.7.16

MOTILAL NEHRU
the patriarch

As is well known, the 1857 uprising affected many people and left behind a bitter legacy. It was not easy to find a safe haven at that time. But Gangadhar (Motilal's father) and his family found one in Agra. Other Kashmiri Brahmin families, who had served the Mughal court, followed them. One of these was Pandit Ajudhia Nath Kunzru's family. His father had settled in Agra, the site of the Sadr Diwani Adalat. In 1866, this court became the High Court. A year later, the High Court was transferred to Allahabad. That is when Ajudhia Nath made the move to live there, along with the Nehrus and the Saprus. Ajudhia Nath went on to become a leading pleader in Allahabad during the 1880s and editor of *Indian Herald* (1879-82), and was also the city's foremost Congress activist.

The family origins of Bishambhar Nath, another Allahabad pleader, were also in Delhi. After 1857, he joined the famous Delhi College and became a part of a Kashmiri group that included Motilal Katju, Dharm Narain Haksar, Sarup Narain Haksar, great grandfather of P.N. Haksar, the renowned civil servant, and Ram Kishen.

Many of the stories of 1857 have survived, but the historian has not paid sufficient attention to the fugitives and their pangs of hunger and thirst. From among those who fled Delhi, the tales of

Ramchander, the mathematician teacher at Delhi College, are well known. Jawaharlal, who knew that the world of the Nehrus first began to darken after the British occupation of Delhi in September, narrated their experience in his *Autobiography*:

> The family, having lost nearly all it possessed, joined the numerous fugitives who were leaving the old imperial city and went to Agra. My father was not born then but my two uncles were already young men and possessed some knowledge of English. This knowledge saved the younger of the two uncles, as well as some other members of the family, from a sudden and ignominious end. He was journeying from Delhi with some family members, among whom was his young sister, a little girl who was very fair, as some Kashmiri children are. Some English soldiers met them on the way and they suspected this little aunt of mine to be an English girl and accused my uncle of kidnapping her. From an accusation, to summary justice and punishment, was usually a matter of minutes in those days, and my uncles and others of the family might well have found themselves hanging on the nearest tree. Fortunately for them, my uncle's knowledge of English delayed matters a little and then someone who knew him passed that way and rescued him and the others.

We know why Motilal's father Gangadhar, then only thirty years old, left Delhi. What we do not know is why he chose to live in Agra, a relatively economically backward city owing to decades of neglect. Yet, he appeared to be doing well until his

Facing page: 'What single family in India can boast of such a galaxy of intellect among its scions as the Nehru family', wrote Motilal to his brother Bansidhar. Motilal (seated middle) with the boys who went to England to be educated. Standing: Jawaharlal, Jivan Lal Katju, Shridhar. Seated: Brijlal, Motilal and Kishenlal.

Below and facing page: Early photographs of Motilal. Another great Indian, Rabindranath Tagore, shared his birthday with him—they were both born on 6 May 1861.

star set as suddenly as it rose. He died in February 1861, barely four years after leaving Delhi and only three months after his wife gave birth to Motilal on 6 May. His premature death came as a bombshell, but Nandlal and Bansidhar, the other two sons, although still in their teens, shouldered family responsibilities and looked after their young brother. Nandlal served Rajputana's Khetri State as its Diwan before resigning in 1870. He qualified as a lawyer and started his practice in Agra. Patient and hard working, he sometimes gave others the impression of being a laborious plodder. That he was not. He worked quietly, steadily, placidly, but with unfailing thoroughness.

Allahabad had been an important administrative division under Akbar, the Mughal emperor. It became the provincial government's seat in 1858 and the seat of the High Court in March 1866. These were the principal reasons that led Nandlal and other Kashmiri Pandit families, along with the *prabasi* Bengalis, the Kayasthas, the Muslim elite, and the local or émigré Brahmins, to avail of the opportunities within the local administrative system. Initially, they encountered difficulties because the British monopolized the Civil Service and because competition for government jobs was fierce. Gradually, however, young and enterprising pleaders or *vakils* performed well because litigation in the 1870s increased considerably. Up to 1870, UP had four advocates and thirty *vakils*. During 1891–1900, their numbers increased to 100 and 235, respectively. Some, like Ajudhia Nath, whose position was consolidated by gradual but incessant effort, benefited from the large number of lucrative land cases that came from Allahabad's rural areas and southern Awadh. Most of the litigants came from the service communities that had once been tied to the expansive Mughal administrative apparatus.

Motilal's early career received nurturing in the home of Nandlal, sixteen years his senior, and his wife, Nandrani. Along with other subjects, he studied Persian, Arabic, and Urdu under Qazi Sadruddin. His earliest impressions were received at the feet of Muslim professors and teachers. These stayed. Luck favoured him in another way. For a city that had its share of religious orthodoxies, caste taboos did not exist in Nandlal's house. Unlike the famous lawyer Bishambhar Nath, who opposed sea voyages, Nandlal's sons—Bijju (Brijlal) Nehru, the

Bansidhar, the eldest brother of Motilal, rose to become a subordinate judge in the judicial service. Unlike his youngest brother he strictly adhered to traditional rituals and did not allow even his children to be present when he ate his meals.

Below: Motilal's diary entry from 31 May 1913—the day Bansidhar passed away.

first Kashmiri member of the 'Superior Governing class', and Kishenlal—were sent to Great Britain; the former studied at Oxford before entering the finance department; the latter obtained a medical degree from Edinburgh. Again, unlike another Kashmiri notable, Jagmohan Nath Chak, who had to perform *prayashchit*—that is, eat cow dung—for going abroad, much to the disgust of Jawaharlal, then at Cambridge, Nandlal's children escaped this 'hocus-pocus'.

Motilal showed early signs of stubborn independence. After returning from his first trip to Europe in 1899, he did not indulge in the tomfoolery of *prayashchit*.

Nandlal and his wife Nandrani. Nandlal began as a teacher in the state of Khetri and ended up as its Diwan or Prime Minister. He died at the age of forty-two leaving the responsibility of bringing up his five sons and one daughter on Motilal.

'No,' he said, 'not even if I die for it.' He was being asked to abandon his entire *Weltanschauung*. That he was not prepared to do. This crusading fervour came to him naturally. He treated with contempt the news of his excommunication from his caste. After all, he was Motilal, the first to adopt 'Nehru' as a surname.

A progressive and artistic home environment helped Motilal deal with social inhibitions and religious sanctions. Allahabad's Muir Central College, then at the height of its fame, unfolded for him a vigorous life, cheerful, optimistic, and earnest. Here, Motilal studied with British teachers like Augustus Harrison and W.H. Wright, learnt his first lessons in British history, culture and contemporary politics, and gained acquaintance of

the nuances of a society whose core values he admired, like many educated Indians of his generation did. Few teachers could ever have had so many pupils who were later to achieve distinction and who bore so clearly the stamp of their masters. Motilal, however, was not an ideal student. More interested in games, he did not study much, a trait his son too developed while a student at Trinity College, Cambridge. But Motilal shared Muir College's enlightened regime with many others. One of these was Mukhtar Ahmad Ansari, who became his doctor and chaired the Congress session in 1927. As Ansari was not one of those people who talked for the sake of talking, his words carried weight. For his part, Ansari, trained in Edinburgh, always counted

Facing page: Motilal with wife Swarup Rani. Married in his teens, his first wife and son had died during childbirth. The beautiful Swarup Rani from Lahore, of Kashmiri extraction, bore Motilal three children.

The stark contrast in their attire, as seen in this photograph, was in direct relation with their parallel lifestyles in Anand Bhawan: while Motilal preferred a western lifestyle, Swarup Rani adhered to her traditional ways.

Motilal among the most important influences of his political life.

Meanwhile, a storm was brewing. Nandlal died of cholera in April 1887 at the age of forty-two, leaving behind an extended family of his widow and six children. Motilal, only twenty-five, himself had no children at this stage; his first wife and their baby had died while Swarup Rani, the second wife, also a Pandit whose family had left Kashmir two generations back, had yet to have a child. Whether Motilal was affected psychologically by this misfortune is not clear, but he responded to the challenge handsomely. As he observed on 4 December 1905, when faced with another personal tragedy, the death of Jawaharlal's infant brother: 'Unmixed and uninterrupted happiness is not given to the spirit which inhabits mortal clay and the true lesson of life lies in making proper use of one's misfortunes. Let us take them as warnings to help to chasten our lower nature and attune the higher self to the "still small voice within" which is seldom heeded except on occasions like this.'

That he did. He was not a man to let grass grow under his feet. Always faithful to his wide intellectual interests—and that included reading and reciting Persian and Urdu poetry—his drive was unabated till the end. His portrait presents a vigorous man, with the clear-cut and domineering mask of a Roman senator. Apart from building his own career that began with an apprenticeship, the strong family feeling that ran in his marrow led him to look after his not-so-well-to-do relatives. He was acutely aware in day-to-day-life of the public duty of being a Nehru. In fact, a strong sense that one's duty to oneself entailed duty to others ran through the Nehrus.

Motilal showed such concern for Shridhar, Bansidhar's son, and advised him 'to go through it (ICS) without losing sight of the one object of his ambition, i.e., to enlighten humanity'. Earlier, on 8 August 1905, he had written to Jawaharlal, the object of his unceasing devotion and attention: 'It will be a proud day for me when I shall have the satisfaction of seeing you a full blown ICS & Kishen [lal] an IMS (Indian Medical Service).' Soon, of course, he changed his mind and preferred, instead, a career for his son at the Bar that offered the highest position and rank to its deserving members. He felt confident of his son rising 'in his father's profession'. Typically, Shridhar's initial failure to clear the ICS (he subsequently succeeded) confirmed his belief that the selectors were 'actuated by political motives in selecting candidates', and that he would shake heaven and earth to expose them.

⌐⌐

Jawaharlal was born on 14 November 1889, a hundred years after the storming of the Bastille, which took place in 1789 and began the French Revolution.

In his younger days, a melancholy hovered about Jawaharlal, everybody's favourite, even as he did his best, usually with success, to cope with life in Anand Bhawan. His was a pampered childhood owing to the father's indulgence and the mother's care and affection: 'an only son of prosperous parents is apt to be spoilt, especially in India,' Jawaharlal wrote in his *Autobiography*. In England, he showed signs of the effects which a distinctly exceptional education produced, though there were no hints yet of greatness in the spheres in which he would excel—

Motilal (seated in front) enjoyed hunting trips with friends—he would travel with an entourage of coolies and cooks. A young Jawaharlal can be seen in the back row perched on a step ladder.

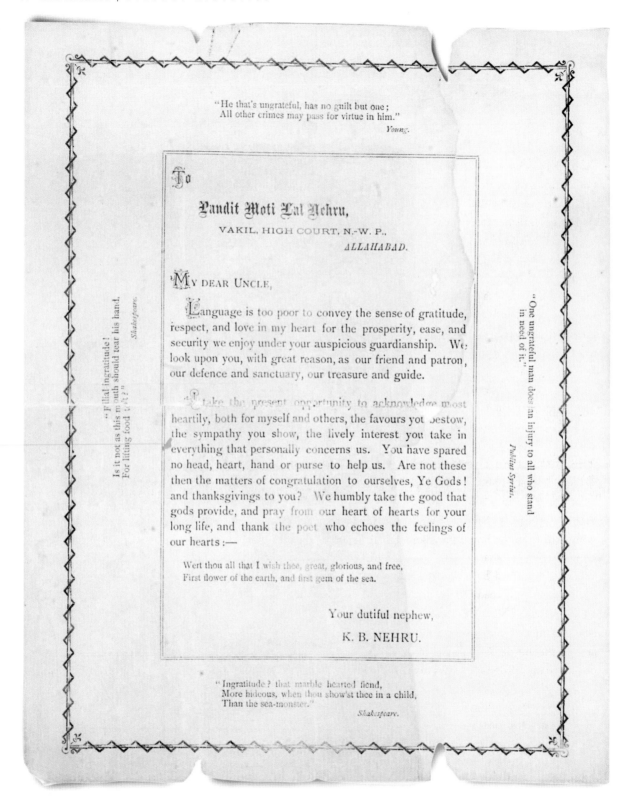

"He that's ungrateful, has no guilt but one;
All other crimes may pass for virtue in him."

Young.

To

Pandit Moti Lal Nehru,

VAKIL, HIGH COURT, N.-W. P.,

ALLAHABAD.

MY DEAR UNCLE,

Language is too poor to convey the sense of gratitude, respect, and love in my heart for the prosperity, ease, and security we enjoy under your auspicious guardianship. We look upon you, with great reason, as our friend and patron, our defence and sanctuary, our treasure and guide.

I take the present opportunity to acknowledge most heartily, both for myself and others, the favours you bestow, the sympathy you show, the lively interest you take in everything that personally concerns us. You have spared no head, heart, hand or purse to help us. Are not these then the matters of congratulation to ourselves, Ye Gods! and thanksgivings to you? We humbly take the good that gods provide, and pray from our heart of hearts for your long life, and thank the poet who echoes the feelings of our hearts :—

Wert thou all that I wish thee, great, glorious, and free,
First flower of the earth, and first gem of the sea.

Your dutiful nephew,

K. B. NEHRU.

"Ingratitude? that marble hearted fiend,
More hideous, when thou show'st thee in a child,
Than the sea-monster."

Shakespeare.

"Filial ingratitude!
Is it not as this mouth should tear his hand,
For lifting food to't?"

Shakespeare.

"One ungrateful man does an injury to all who stand in need of it."

Publius Syrius.

Kishenlal's letter of gratitude to uncle Motilal.

Sarup Kumari (later Vijaya Lakshmi Pandit) with Krishna Kumari in 1911. Sarup Kumari, born on 18 August 1900, was the first girl to be born in the Nehru family after nine boys. Krishna Kumari was born seven years later while Jawaharlal was still in England.

leadership and statesmanship. He had adapted to the conventions of Harrow, the famous British public school he joined in the Christmas term of 1905 at the age of sixteen. After his two-year stay at Harrow, he would have liked to stay on for another year, and was sorry to leave the school for good. In Trinity College, Cambridge, he found a stimulus—lectures and debates—to the busy exercise of a very independent mind. In his letters, he gave the impression of being intimately acquainted with the university's history and having a punctilious regard for its traditions.

In June 1912, Jawaharlal was called to the Bar. In autumn he returned home after having stayed in England for over seven years. The contrast with Cambridge's cloistered world could not have been starker. For a while he found the 'utter insipidity of life' disconcerting, but he soon discovered fun and excitement around him. After the stuffiness of Trinity College, talking to friends and interacting with visitors to the house was like fresh air from an opened window. Anand Bhawan itself came alive. Vijaya Lakshmi had the time to go horseriding with her brother, and read, for example, the works of George Bernard Shaw. The reading habits Jawaharlal acquired in his younger days did not change even amidst the hustle and bustle of political life. He described his passion for books in the following way: 'They stand there, row after row, with the wisdom of ages locked up in them, serene and untroubled in a changing and distracted world, looking down silently on the mortals that come and go.' His fondness for Vijaya Lakshmi, too, remained. In his eloquent will, he recorded: 'In the course of a life which has had its share of trial and difficulty, the love and tender care for me of both my sisters, Vijaya

Lakshmi Pandit and Krishna Hutheesing, has been of the greatest solace to me.'

Motilal was overjoyed that his son was back in the midst of his family with a new career and, in some fundamental respects, a new attitude to life. Once, after returning from a long trip in Europe, he had expressed 'the firm conviction that I have sown the seed of your future greatness and I have not the shadow of a doubt that you have a great career before you'. Similarly, he took pride in Vijaya Lakshmi. 'You are a brave little darling,' he told her

On a hunting expedition. On the far left is Motilal's nephew Brijlal Nehru, Swarup Rani is seated in the middle holding a gun, next to her is Brijlal's elder son Brij Kumar (B.K. Nehru). Seated next to him is Sarup Kumari. Jawaharlal can be seen standing behind them. Motilal is standing second from the right.

'The scene of my labors.' Motilal sent this postcard of the Allahabad High Court to Jawaharlal. A lawyer with a flourishing legal practice, he is said to have refused an offer of £1,000 from a client because he did not feel up to it.

on 19 January 1919, 'I was remarking last night at the dinner table that you alone of my children have inherited my spirit.' It was this fusion of professional commitment and family pride he bequeathed to his son and elder daughter.

The search for a 'faultless' bride for Jawaharlal began, much to his displeasure and resentment, in 1906. Ultimately, he acquiesced to marrying the 'Delhi girl', of a 'typically fair skin of Brahmins of Kashmiri descent'. At the time of the marriage he was twenty-six, and Kamala was seventeen. Motilal had more exhilarating news when his daughter-in-

law gave birth to a child on 19 November 1917. *Mubarak ho Bhai and Bhabi Saheb,*' the family Munshi prayed. 'May Allah's blessings go with the child, who should be a worthy heir to Jawahar as Jawahar has proved a worthy son to you, and may the child illuminate the name of Jawaharlal Nehru.' However, not a grandson, as Munshiji thought, but a granddaughter was born. She was named Indira. 'This girl is going to be worth more than a thousand grandsons,' the grandfather prophesied.

Professionally for Motilal, work was flowing in from all directions. In 1896, at the age of thirty-five,

Motilal was largely responsible for the family's fortune.
His wealth was not so much inherited as re-earned,
in a profession that had come to acquire great importance
and respect.

Motilal earned Rs 2,000 a month; by 1905, his income had increased four-fold. His clients included begums and ranis, who would come to Anand Bhawan in a curtained car or an elaborate horse carriage and enter Motilal's study to sit behind the screen. The Lakhna estate case yielded rich rewards. So did the Dumraon case that dragged on for years. Motilal joined battle with C.R. Das, the charismatic lawyer from Bengal and co-founder of the Swaraj Party. They crossed swords in court but met in the evening over drinks. Motilal was taken to be a magician, especially after being one of the four to receive the status and privilege of 'Advocates of the Allahabad High Court' in 1896. 'To my mind,' he observed on 7 November 1905, 'it is simple enough. I want money, I work for it and I get it.' He had plenty of it. People remembered the occasions when he would go to Lucknow on a case for one of the big *taluqdar*s. The retinue that travelled with him was second to no prince. He reached the pinnacle of success not by seeking anyone's favour, but through hard work, intelligence and intellect.

꧂

Only Indians lived in the crowded Chowk Mirganj area with its narrow roads, winding lanes, open drains, and ill-ventilated houses. That is where Motilal had a house. In 1900, he moved to the Civil Lines, an exclusive residential area where members of the British elite lived in an ordered environment, in spacious houses enclosed by large gardens and joined by wide, straight roads. Motilal decorated his new house with expensive European artifacts that he had picked up during his travels. Although stories of his linen being washed in Paris and his Sauterne from France were apocryphal, a governess moved in for the young children, knives and forks appeared on the dining table, and social conversation veered mostly around Shakespeare and the great nineteenth-century romantic poets. Once, Motilal purchased a set of Bohemian glasses, the kind just bought by King Edward VII. 'Who in Allahabad is going to appreciate these,' asked Swarup Rani, who was by now accustomed to her husband's princely habits, 'and why should we be like King Edward?'

On another occasion, M.R. Jayakar, Bombay's lawyer and legislator, asked him about the tilt in his khaddar cap, as it sat on his forehead, and the reason why it looked different from that of other wearers. To this, he remarked, 'you have to be born a Kashmiri to know this, a rugged Maratha like you can hardly understand this business.'

Motilal, Swarup Rani and their daughter Sarup Kumari at her fifth birthday party in Bad Ems, Germany, 1905. After admitting Jawaharlal to Harrow the family travelled around Europe. Motilal hosted a sumptuous tea party for Sarup Kumari's birthday to which he invited 400 children from neighbouring schools. Due to his extremely successful legal practice, Motilal could afford certain luxuries and was known to run a lavish household. He was a generous host and would throw extravagant parties where he entertained both European and Indian society.

From

       The Hon'ble Mr. J. W. Hose, I.C.S.,

       Chief Secretary to Government,

       United Provinces.

To

       The Hon'ble Pandit Moti Lal Nehru,

       of Allahabad.

Political)
Department.) Sir,

           Dated Allahabad, 22 November 1911.

    I am directed by His Honour the Lieutenant Governor to inform you that you have been selected as one of the provincial representatives of the United Provinces to do homage to Their Imperial Majesties the King Emperor and Queen Empress on the occasion of the Coronation Durbar on the 12th December 1911.

      I have the honour to be,

          Sir,

      Your most obedient servant,

          for Chief Secretary.

Left: Letter inviting Motilal to the Coronation Durbar in Delhi in 1911.

Below: A smartly dressed Motilal.

Bottom: Motilal in his car—the first to be seen in Allahabad. Sarup Kumari, wearing a large bonnet, is seated on his lap.

Facing page: Family portrait. Front row: Jawaharlal. Middle row: Lado Rani Zutshi, Motilal, Swarup Rani. Last row: Rameshwari Nehru, her husband Brijlal Nehru and Lillian Hooper, the Nehru girls' English governess.

Facing page: Gandhi once said that Motilal's most striking quality was the love for his son—his love for India was derived from his love for Jawaharlal. When Jawaharlal took over as Congress President from him in 1929, Motilal quoted a Persian saying, 'What the father cannot achieve, the son does.'

Watching his butler serve him a dish of eggs, an orthodox Hindu visitor remarked in horror, 'Panditji, you are not going to eat those eggs!' 'I most certainly am,' was the reply, 'and in another few moments I am going to eat their mother too.'

Like most of his contemporaries, Motilal was cut off from the common man, and the lifestyle in Anand Bhawan was truly out of sync with that of most Indian professionals. Still, he followed the debates in Congress circles on poverty, unemployment and social degradation, without reacting specifically to the views of Dadabhai Naoroji, R.C. Dutt and other early Indian nationalists.

Motilal argued that the people's credulity and irrationalism was the greatest threat to civilization. This could be overcome only by encouraging people to question and doubt the things they are told by politicians and priests. Unlike his son, who believed that capitalism negated justice, freedom and democracy, Motilal claimed that a class war triggered by Bolshevik ideas would jettison India's progress. He was not the only one to air such apprehensions. A fierce controversy raged over the impact of the Russian revolution (1917) and the significance of Marxian ideas in the 1920s. To admire Karl Marx and Lenin was to identify oneself with a rebellion against conventional standards of propriety, to ally oneself with a movement that rejected religion, and to preach class war. Motilal insisted that the masses wanted bread and had 'no time to make experiments and no use for theories and dogmas imported from abroad'. He stated his credo at the Amritsar Congress session in December 1919:

We must aim at an India where all are free and have the fullest opportunities of development, where women have ceased to be in bondage, and the rigours of the caste system have disappeared; where there are no privileged classes or communities; where education is free and open to all; where capitalists and the landlords do not oppress the labourer and the *raiyat*; where labour is respected and well paid, and poverty, the nightmare of the present generation, is a thing of the past.

All his life Motilal had been conscious of his own place in history. At the same time everything in his life was arranged around his desire to bring up a son and to see him grow up to be the pride of his father. When he was leaving the young Jawahar at Harrow, he wrote a like a true patriarch:

You must bear in mind that in you we are leaving the dearest treasure we have in this world and perhaps in other worlds to come.... It is not a question of providing for you as I can do that perhaps in one single year's income. It is a question of making a real man of you which you are bound to be. It would have been extremely selfish—I should say sinful—to keep you with us and leave you a fortune in gold with little or no education. I think I can without vanity say that I am the founder of the fortunes of the Nehru family. I look upon you, my dear son, as the man who will build upon the foundations I have laid and have the satisfaction of seeing a noble structure of renown rearing up its head to the skies.

As in other matters, Motilal Nehru's instincts were based on the confidence that for an aristocratic family like his all things were possible, and that he had played his part in preparing his son for a role in running the world.

Motilal donated the old Anand Bhawan, later renamed Swaraj Bhawan, to the Congress Party in 1930. It was the first house in Allahabad to have a swimming pool, electricity and running water.

Background: The original blueprint of the old Anand Bhawan.

Facing page: A hub of constant activity, the new Anand Bhawan became the home of the extended Nehru family and those involved in the nationalist movement. In 1942, Lal Bahadur Shastri (later Prime Minister of India) hid from the British in a room at Anand Bhawan. The servants were told that he was an ailing Nehru relative while Indira Gandhi brought him his meals.

Among the many graphic descriptions of Allahabad, a gracious town, the one from Vijaya Lakshmi Pandit's personal memoir is worth quoting:

There were long tree-lined avenues, well-laid-out public gardens, and large houses standing in the midst of smooth green lawns. It is known for its High Court, where many stars of the legal profession practised and made great names for themselves. The university with its sprawling campus held prestigious position in the province. The town was divided into the English and the Indian quarters, and only comparatively few Indians could afford to live in the Civil Lines, as the English sector was called. The Civil Lines had an English shopping centre where British goods, particularly wearing apparel, were available. There was a beautiful park named for Prince Khusru, and Company Bagh, called after the East India Company, where a military band played Western music every Saturday, and people drove out in their smart carriages to take the air and listen to the music. The benches in this park were marked 'for Europeans Only' and for this reason were not used. The 'Europeans,' or, rather, the wives of the British officials, sat in their carriages, and the few Indians who went to the park would not risk an insult so walked around the garden or sat on the grass.

They say that houses have the corporate soul of their inhabitants. Anand Bhawan was one such house. To Jawaharlal, it was far more than a structure of brick and concrete, or a private possession: it was connected intimately with the freedom struggle, and within its walls great events occurred and great decisions were taken.

From the verandah one could look out on a great expanse of garden full of gladioli, daffodils, sweet peas, and roses. Hundreds of birds flitted

about, adding their sweet songs and colour to its beauty. No wonder that, from her childhood, Indira Nehru looked upon trees as life giving and a refuge. She loved climbing and hiding in trees, in a little place that was her own.

Motilal moved his family to this forty-two-room house in 1900. A judge of the Allahabad High Court had built this house before Motilal bought it. Living in it was an experience not because one looked out over the world from lofty isolation but because one saw new faces amidst all the hustle and bustle. And the house was always open to the extended Nehru family. Motilal wanted Bansidhar, his brother, to share the good life: 'Indeed you have not seen the younger generation of Nehrus which came into existence after you left Allahabad [for Agra]. They should have a chance of seeing the head of the family and it goes without saying that you will be right heartily welcome to all.'

B.K. Nehru, son of Motilal's nephew Brijlal Nehru and his wife, Rameshwari, who edited a Hindi women's magazine *Stri Darpan*, was born on 4 September 1909 in a room at the extreme northwest corner of Anand Bhawan. People referred to him as Bijju. He had an interesting story to tell about the 'very strong elements of nationalism'. Once, Rameshwari Nehru wrote to Jawaharlal in Harrow telling him to return home and work towards the end of colonial rule. The letter reached the Head Master. He opened it, read its revolutionary message, and wanted to know the identity of the fiery young lady who wrote the treasonable letter. She turned out to be Jawaharlal's very young sister-in-law.

There was nothing bohemian about the Nehrus' way of life, and their place in the upper reaches of Indian society was confidently assumed. It was a life that combined the benefits of privilege with the satisfaction of participating in the freedom movement; the freedom from caste and religious conventions with the confidence and assurance of belonging to a long and proud tradition.

Anand Bhawan hosted relatives, friends and comrades in the spacious and specially furnished rooms for weeks and months. 'We are full up here…,' Jawaharlal informed Indira on 6 April 1936, 'overfull with guests. Bapu and Ba [Kasturba Gandhi] and Mahadeva [Desai] and four others of their party. And Vallabhbhai [Patel] and his daughter. And Mrs. [Sarojini] Naidu and Padmaja [Naidu]. Betty [Krishna Hutheesing] and Raja [her husband, G.P. Hutheesing] are here also with their two kids…' More guests came during fairs, exhibitions and *melas*, such as the Kumbh Mela that was held every twelve years. 'It is *mela* time,' Jawaharlal told Indira on 14 January 1938, 'and crowds of pilgrims are streaming into Anand Bhawan.'

Motilal stood out in every society. He was also the perfect host. Jovial, easygoing and generous, he entertained friends and relatives lavishly, serving them drinks, cigarettes, and Awadhi cuisine. They played tennis, enjoyed the spacious garden, sat around the tiered fountain in the centre of the courtyard, or took a dip in the indoor swimming pool. Most of Motilal's friendships lasted; many played a significant part in his professional, political or private life. Friends loved him for his searching, lucid and incisive mind, but they also criticized him for being too worldly, domineering, acerbic, willful—flaws of character which, in their way, were redeemed by his gracious and courteous bearing. There were those who were captivated by his aristocratic manner, his humour tempered with good taste in Urdu and Persian poetry, and his

sophistication, which under no circumstances degenerated into 'showing off'.

Once, he told an uncle: 'You may not dine with me without polluting yourself, but I suppose we could share whisky and soda?' Now and then the young Jawaharlal, who spent much of his time with his tutors and mother, would peep at the guests from behind a curtain. If he were caught he would be dragged out and made to sit on his father's knee. He and the servants often faced his uncontrollable temper. When that happened, he would rush to mother Swarup Rani. She had been married at fourteen, when Motilal was already an adult. 'She was,' her daughter Vijaya Lakshmi wrote, 'an extremely beautiful person—dainty like an ivory carving with lovely hazel eyes, exquisite hands and feet and thick chestnut hair that fell in waves far below her waist and which we loved to brush and play with.'

On one occasion, his father beat up Jawaharlal for stealing one of his fountain pens, driving him 'almost blind with pain and mortification at my disgrace'. As before, he rushed to his mother, and for several days various creams and ointments were applied to his aching and quivering body. On another occasion, when he saw his father drink claret or a deep red wine, he hurried to tell her, 'Father is drinking blood.' Swarup Rani lived in the western wing of the house, where she retained her orthodox ways. Quiet and dignified, she hosted political leaders as well, who gathered on Anand Bhawan's southern side. To support her in running the house, she had her sister, Bibi Amma, a child widow. Such was the closeness between the two sisters that Bibi Amma (Rajpati Kaul) died of a brain haemorrhage less than 24 hours after Swarup Rani passed away in January 1938. Even though Anand Bhawan's inmates were wary of Bibi Amma's petty intrigues, they tolerated her presence. The gentle Kamala Nehru, in particular, suffered at her hands.

In the Christmas week of December 1885, a small group of social reformers, journalists, lawyers and publicists gathered to act as mediators between the government and the 'advanced' Indian public opinion. They were dismissed, in official circles, as a 'microscopic minority'. But the same small group became the catalyst for a major political agitation headed by the Indian National Congress. The chief architect of the newly-born party was Allan Octavian Hume. These were big men making history. Today, their names are inscribed on public monuments and the saga of their sacrifices is recorded in textbooks. Motilal, then a young lawyer in Kanpur, attended the 1888 Congress session at Allahabad. It was a bewildering but also a wonderful experience. Soon, he found a place in the Subjects Committee, along with Surendranath Banerjee, Gopal Krishna Gokhale, and Pandit Madan Mohan Malaviya, one of the founders of the Prayag Hindu Samaj and the UP Hindu Sabha. In 1892, he hosted the Congress session in Allahabad.

Already in the throes of much nationalist activity, Allahabad appeared on India's political map. The People's Association's early initiatives had turned the city into a hunting ground for local, regional and national leaders. Bal Gangadhar Tilak, a leader who had acquired countrywide fame for his anti-British crusade, delivered fiery speeches in Allahabad in 1907. Gokhale, also a Chitpavan Brahmin from Poona but Tilak's *bête noire*, lectured

in the city in the first week of February. The enthusiasm generated by his visit was such that students drew his carriage amidst the deafening cries of *Bande Mataram*. Japan's victory over Russia in 1905 had already stirred the young. For Jawaharlal, it was a trend that perfectly matched his mood of rejoicing in a sense of liberation from the past, and he took great delight in the affront to a Western country that Japan's victory represented. Speaking for himself and his friends, he wrote that 'both individual and national honour demanded a more aggressive and fighting attitude to foreign rule.'

By the 1890s, the Congress was beginning to garner more support than it had ever done before, and many influential men began to move closer to it. Motilal was not one of them. A rather marginal figure for at least a decade after 1892, the year the Congress met in Allahabad, he was excluded from its policy decisions and remained somewhat distant from its leadership. There was little sign of anyone wooing him into becoming more closely involved, or that he himself wanted to do so. His own work kept him occupied and he had no overpowering impulse to get embroiled in the great political issues of the day. His son, on the other hand, had made his political debut with a speech in Allahabad on 20 June 1916 to protest against the Press Act. Later, he took an active interest in the Home Rule League, founded by the British Theosophist Annie Besant.

Slowly, however, the quickening pulse of politics brought Motilal closer to public life, as a Congress activist. Once that happened he began spreading his net wider. Students followed his lead. He, in turn, took them as he found them, was solicitous about them, and would talk with them for hours. Young lawyers and journalists struggling to

Facing page: In the early years Motilal was more of an observer than a participant in politics. He chose to support the 'moderates' (to the disapproval of his young son), who were led by Gopal Krishna Gokhale.

make a career looked upon him as a trusted guide. He took them under his wing. His willingness to place his knowledge and experience at their disposal did not fail; some remembered receiving more attention than they deserved.

Motilal was not a firebrand agitator. The man who had worked very hard to build his practice knew the hazards of spewing venom against the British government, courting arrest, or boycotting British goods. Even after the unruffled acceptance of arrest, prosecution and prison, he painfully recorded Jawahar boarding a third-class railway compartment: 'this is a time when he should be enjoying himself, but he has given up everything and has become a *sadhu*.' Moreover, he abhorred fuss and rhetoric of the kind that came into play at the time of the swadeshi *andolan* against Bengal's partition. He approved neither the grand spectacle of *dhotis* and *chaddars* nor the ascendancy of the extremists, a disparate but highly vocal group within the Congress that spurned British rule and desired its overthrow with bombs and bullets. Nor did he support their style and method. On 27 December 1906, he made it clear that his province would vote against the decision of the extremists to notify the government to quit and hand over the reins of government to the 'oily' babus.

As for British rule, he stated explicitly at the UP provincial conference held in Allahabad on 29 March 1907 that, 'John Bull means well—it is not in his nature to mean ill....' He may not have gone to the extent of regarding British rule as the fortuitous dispensation of divine providence, a view aired by early nationalists like Dadabhai Naoroji, Gokhale and Pherozeshah Mehta, but he could not see eye to eye with the extremist path chosen by Tilak, Lajpat Rai,

B.C. Pal, and Aurobindo Ghose to win freedom. For him the alarm bells rang after Tilak's revolutionary speech at the Muir College in late January 1907. In theory, the two approaches conflicted; in practice, they resulted in a difference of emphasis.

The young Jawaharlal had been alerted gradually to nationalist movements in Ireland and India. Then, in February and March 1905, the Japanese inflicted heavy defeats on Russia's land forces in Manchuria at Mukden. Jawaharlal sent a postcard to Brijlal in 1905 saying simply, 'Three cheers for Togo,' a reference to the annihilation of Russia's European Baltic battle fleet at the battle of Tsushima on 27 May 1905. He wanted 'a little stirring up', especially after discovering that the voice of the moderates was little more than a whisper in the newspapers. His father's 'immoderately moderate' tone made Jawaharlal uncomfortable. On 30 June 1908, he wrote to him: 'The government must be feeling very pleased with you at your attitude. I wonder if the insulting offer of a Rai Bahadurship, or something equivalent to it, would make you less of a moderate than you are.' Some of these letters reveal that Jawaharlal had already chosen the ground from which he was never to move during his ever-widening survey of history and politics. His son's sharp comments irked Motilal, who told him sternly, 'You know me and my views well enough to understand that I do not approve of the opinion expressed by you.'

Biographers tend to exaggerate the effect of Cambridge, but it did encourage in Jawaharlal the spirit of questioning and dissent. At the same time, there was nothing iconoclastic about his radicalism, and it involved no split between father and son. When tried on 17 May 1922 by K.N. Knox,

Allahabad's district magistrate, Jawaharlal stated: 'I looked upon the world almost from an Englishman's standpoint. And so I returned [from England] to India as much prejudiced in favour of England and the English as it was possible for an Indian to be.' Indeed, he was not the stuff of which iconoclasts are made.

The fact is that Motilal was too self-willed and proud a man to ingratiate himself with senior government officials. Nor was he the kind to hanker after honours. He believed that the road to freedom was strewn with difficulties, and that its ultimate attainment depended on Indians learning the art of self-government step by step. He pinned faith in English institutions, and having established warm contact with several Liberal leaders during his visits to England in 1899, 1900, 1905 and 1909, he found them to be committed to some form of Indian representation on legislative bodies. That is why he backed the Lucknow Pact of December 1916, which reflected a broad consensus on the major issues of Indian representation in the decision-making bodies. It was a consensus hammered out by the Congress and Muslim League leaders, notably Tilak and Mohammad Ali Jinnah, the future founder of Pakistan. In Motilal's view, a Hindu-Muslim front and the building up of moderate public opinion would leave a powerful impression on the government.

It must be said that Motilal's faith in the government's sensitivity to nationalistic aspirations rested on ill-founded assumptions. The Act of 1909 had not offered much to satisfy even the moderates; the Act of 1919, too, fell short of the Lucknow demands. At the same time, Motilal was not the only one to pin his hopes on the generosity of the rulers and their appreciation of Congress demands. Early Indian nationalism had been relatively free of anti-colonial rhetoric, and the Congress platform frequently debated whether to trust, as the moderates vouchsafed, the British government or go the extremist way. This resulted in the Surat split in 1907.

The Congress wind blew hot and cold after Surat. Some vacillated; others searched for a satisfactory programme of political action of their own. Motilal, for his part, buttressed the claims of the moderates. On 7 February 1919, he launched *The Independent* at Anand Bhawan. The paper would 'think aloud for India', he declared. Although he trod the political ladder wearily, he did not buckle under pressure. He courted the storm on several occasions and braved it to the best of his ability: 'the greater the opposition the merrier it is for me,' he had once written when a local newspaper fulminated against him. His refusal to undergo the purification ceremony after returning from Europe had reflected the same defiant spirit. He told a family friend, 'I will ruthlessly and mercilessly lay bare the tattered fabric of its (caste) existence and tear it into the minutest possible shreds.' Strong words but spoken with conviction.

Motilal's easy ways or his pro-British proclivities did not deter him from lambasting the government. In the Provincial Legislative Council, to which he was elected in 1910, his reputation rested on being the government's outspoken critic. This criticism in April 1910 excited 'the anger of the Gods'. Annie Besant's internment in June 1917 led him to raise aloft the banner of Home Rule League, a body formed to grab public attention. His younger colleagues and admirers responded by energizing the Allahabad Home Rule League. They were: Manzar Ali Sokhta, who lived in Anand Bhawan until he was asked to leave owing to his radical activities;

Motilal, known to possess an incisive intellect, ready wit, and a combative spirit as a lawyer, had the confidence of a self-made man.

P.D. Tandon, once editor of the Hindi newspaper *Abhuydaya*; Syed Hosain, editor of *The Independent* and a friend of Vijaya Lakshmi; Zahur Ahmad and Kamaluddin Jafri, both lawyers; Abdul Majid Khwaja and T.A.K. Sherwani, Jawaharlal's contemporaries at Cambridge; and Wahid Yah Khan, editor of *Nai Roshni*. Several members of the Nehru family, including Uma Nehru, wife of Shamlal Nehru, Jawaharlal's cousin, and Mohanlal Nehru, also his cousin, jumped into the fray, demanding liberation from colonial bondage. Jawaharlal himself gave notice of a public meeting in Allahabad on 21 June 1917, adding, 'Ours have been the politics of cowards and opium-eaters long enough and it is time we thought and acted like live men and women who place the honour and interests of their country above the frowns and smiles of every Tom, Dick and Harry who has ICS attached to his name.'

Without using such strong words, Motilal believed that in arresting Annie Besant, the authorities had behaved in a unique, and one might say inspired, blend of stupidity and panic. To cap it all, the massacre at the Jallianwala Bagh on 15 April 1919 left him with a different, and much darker, view of British rule. Then, his travels as a member of the Civil Disobedience Enquiry Committee brought him closer to the common people, something that enabled him to see and feel their suffering. On 2 March 1919, he chaired the meeting of the newly formed Allahabad Satyagraha Sabha. At the Amritsar Congress session in 1919, to reinforce his arguments, he cited the Persian verse, 'If a king tolerates one grain of oppression, his retinue will inflict a ton of misery.' His harsh comments were reserved for General Reginald Dyer, the perpetrator of the Jallianwala Bagh tragedy: 'What words, fellow

delegates, can I use to express your feelings and mine whose kith and kin were mercilessly shot down by the hundred in cold blood? Well may we grieve in the words of the Persian poet:

Our country is flooded with sorrow and woe,
O, for our land woe!
Arise and for coffin and cerements go!
O, for our land woe!
With the blood of our men killed in this pursuit
The moon shines red,
Hill, plain, and garden blood-red glow:
O, for our land woe!

Although Motilal and Gandhi did not always agree, they remained close to each other. Jawaharlal described their relationship: 'In the language of psychoanalysis it was a meeting of an introvert with an extrovert. Yet there were common bonds, common interests which drew the two together and kept up, even when, in later years, their politics diverged, a close relationship between them.'

Facing page: Gandhi's letter to Motilal in 1929, indicating that it was time for the young blood in the Congress, led by Jawaharlal, to assume charge. Jawaharlal became Congress President that year.

The last straw was the appointment of an all-white Statutory Commission, intended to determine the pace of constitutional reforms, on 8 November 1927. As Congress president in 1928, Motilal thundered: 'To my mind, the circumstances attending it are symptomatic of a grave organic infection and not merely of the well-known functional incapacity of the Government. It shows the presence of the toxin of Dyerism in their internal economy.' He had once said that pure idealism, completely divorced from realities, had no place in politics and that it was a happy dream that sooner or later ended in a rude awakening. His faith in British rule rudely shaken, he decided to throw his weight behind the major nationalist initiatives. However, as a practical visionary, he changed his public stance from time to time not for any opportunistic reason but because of the changes taking place in Indian politics.

His relationship with Gandhi illustrates this. Their differences sprang largely from the two men's contrasting estimate of political realities. Gandhi, fresh from his satyagraha against the Rowlatt Act, believed that everything was interconnected—the Jallianwala Bagh tragedy, the 'Punjab wrong' and the Khilafat episode. Motilal was less certain that this

Although by the early 1920s, the family was barely ever together at the same time in Allahabad again, the family bonding between the Nehrus continued to be strong. Here Swarup Rani is embraced by her younger daughter Krishna Kumari while Motilal's nephew Shamlal (Arun Nehru's grandfather) springs from behind.

Facing page: Motilal in 1924. Gandhi's visit to Anand Bhawan in 1920 was a turning point for the Nehru family. They became non-cooperators and embraced all the lifestyle changes that brought with it. Motilal, once a connoisseur of the finest Savile Row suits, henceforth only wore traditional clothing made of home-spun cloth.

was so. He was not one to be swept off his feet by any tide of passion. While recognizing satyagraha as a new force in Indian politics, he did not endorse the wording of the satyagraha pledge. Nonetheless, as Indira Gandhi related decades later, 'Jallianwala Bagh was a turning point. This is when the family came much closer to Mahatma Gandhi and our whole way of life changed.'

The change came slowly. Motilal continued to believe that Congressmen were only bound by the principles accepted by the Congress and not by Gandhi's diktat. On non-cooperation, he was by no means sure as to the form it would take in practice; in fact, he stated in February 1920 that Gandhian policies had the potential of leading the country to civil strife. On 16 June 1920, he suggested to Jawaharlal that they should select for themselves

constituencies for the UP Council to which elections were due later in the year.

In this frame of mind he attended the Special Congress session in September 1920. But, as it turned out, he decided to second the non-cooperation resolution. Immediately afterwards, he resigned from the UP Council and announced that he would not seek re-election to the reformed legislature. Jamnadas Dwarkadas, Annie Besant's ardent follower, provides the following version:

> Motilal Nehru, who had come to meet Jinnah at the Howrah station told him in my presence that Gandhiji wanted to pass a non-cooperation resolution and that this would mean boycott of the legislatures and he (Motilal) suggested to Jinnah that all of them together, i.e., Jinnah, Malaviya, C.R. Das, Lajpat Rai, Motilal Nehru, Mrs. Besant and others should combine to defeat the resolution. When the resolution was passed ten or twelve days later, Motilal, influenced by his son Jawaharlal, voted in favour of the resolution along with Gandhi. When the actual voting by poll was decided upon, it was felt that resolution would be defeated, but next day when the poll took place, Umar Sobani and Shankerlal managed to add over a hundred delegates from the streets and got them to vote for the resolution.

The fact is that Motilal could neither ignore the Mahatma's overpowering presence nor his extraordinary influence. This was one reason, and a strong one, for him to join the Khilafat-Non-cooperation bandwagon. There were other reasons as well. He could not continue to be awkwardly placed vis-à-vis his son, who had developed a strong bonding with Gandhi. Lastly, he believed that it was impossible for one part of the Indian people

Motilal with Swarup Rani and Krishna Kumari. Motilal had died when his youngest child married Gonottam Hutheesing (Raja) at Anand Bhawan on 20 October 1933. The marriage with a Jain, was the first in the family outside the Brahmin fold. On 27 October 1933, Jawaharlal wrote to Gandhi, who was consulted on important matters after Motilal's death: 'The idea that Krishna should marry somebody who is not even a Brahmin is more than she (mother) can comfortably swallow...My views about it are the exact opposite of mother's. I would welcome as wide a break from old customs as possible.'

Motilal served two prison terms; first for six months in 1921–22 and then for three months in 1930. In his absence, Anand Bhawan was run according to his instructions which he sent in great detail through letters to various family members. Ladli Prasad Zutshi, Motilal's sister's son, was given formal charge of the household—a role he continued in even after Motilal's death.

to stand aloof while the other part suffered under a serious grievance. This stance itself is quintessentially Motilal: supporting what he believed to be right, unperturbed by the protestations of friends who opposed the mixing of religion with politics, and giving up a flourishing practice for a good cause without the slightest thought to the consequences.

Indeed, when the lid he had put on his political ideas came unstuck, it affected both his personality and his attitude to life fundamentally and permanently. The fundamental importance of this 'conversion' was realized by Motilal at the time. Jawaharlal explained:

> His reason, his strong sense of self-respect, and his pride, all led him step by step to throw in his lot wholeheartedly with the new movement. The accumulated anger with which a series of events, culminating in the Punjab tragedy and its aftermath, filled him; the sense of utter wrong-doing and injustice, the bitterness of national humiliation, had to find some way out. It was only when his reason, backed by the trained mind of a lawyer, had weighed all the pros and cons that he took the final decision and joined Gandhiji in his campaign.

Like Mazharul Haq, his contemporary in Patna, also a renowned lawyer, Motilal changed his style of life, took to swadeshi ways, and went to prison. He was lodged in Lucknow District Jail from 6 December 1921 to 6 June 1922 (transferred to Nainital Jail in May 1922). Swarup Rani, too, donned khadi clothes and went about addressing meetings both in the towns and in adjoining villages. The Spode china and Venetian glass, the stock of choice wines, and the prized horses and dogs were sold. Indira, only three in 1920, watched the bonfire of imported cloth. One day, she climbed up to the terrace and set light to her imported doll. 'The course of events,' Krishna Hutheesing recalled, 'brought a turnabout in the tenor and direction of our family's way of life.' The gay and carefree chitchat of yesteryears became a thing of the past. Once the home of lavish parties, Anand Bhawan now hosted the austere Gandhi,

Motilal and Swarup Rani address a women's gathering.
Jawaharlal wrote about his father: 'His reason, his strong sense
of self-respect, and his pride, all led him step by step to throw
in his lot wholeheartedly with the new movement.'

Vallabhabhai Patel, Ansari, Azad, and the Ali brothers.

It is true that the Mahatma's 'hobbies' did not interest Motilal beyond a certain point. It is also true that, in October 1924, he wrote to Purshotamdas Thakurdas, a Bombay industrialist, apprehending that the Mahatma would either convert the Congress into a spinners' association or else persist with his non-cooperating methods. Worried by his dwindling income, he even threatened to resume the practice of law. But it was unimaginable for him to break from the Congress or to defy Gandhi's supreme leadership. Gandhi, in turn, found him to be a dependable ally, and an ideal choice for the Congress presidency in 1928.

Gandhi had followed Motilal's constructive role in the All Parties Conference and evinced interest in the Nehru Report, named after Motilal, who had

Motilal and Jawaharlal outside Naini Central Prison, Allahabad, after their arrest on 14 April 1930. This was Motilal's last prison term.

chaired the drafting committee. Piloted between the Scylla of Muslim League's hesitation and the Charybdis of nationalist ambitions and impatience as personified by Jawaharlal, the report sought to tackle several complicated issues relating to future governance and representation. The impartial weighing of arguments and counter-arguments, especially on Hindu-Muslim representation, was Motilal's own. Indeed, his personal reputation and standing gave the report a particular quality, a touch of the incredible being made credible, which accounted in part for the disgruntlement of the Ali brothers and the politically conservative Muslim establishment, led by the Aga Khan. Gandhi complimented Motilal, 'without whose effort there would have been no Committee, there would have been no unanimity, and there would have been no report'.

The fact is that Motilal was at his best in a committee, where his legal mind gave him such an advantage, and the responsibility of sagacious counsel lay upon him. Repeatedly, he spoke of 'the natural cravings of the human heart for freedom', and of Swaraj emerging 'from an ordeal of fire unscathed and pure'. He held forth in the Legislative Assembly, a forum he and his Swarajist colleagues used to push forward the national demand. Whenever he did so, it was distilled sense and reason. According to Jayakar, also a member of the assembly, he would enter the Legislature while a debate was on, and proceed, with measured and dignified steps, to occupy his seat on the Opposition benches, all eyes resting on him. 'In all that he did, his innate dignity and self-confidence were his unique attributes.'

Talking of the Assembly, the Motilal-Jinnah

Anand Bhawan.
Allahabad, March 27, 1930.

To The President,
    Indian National Congress,
        Allahabad.

Dear Mr.President,

I am now placing before you formally my proposal to present the old "Anand Bhawan" to the Nation which you and I discussed with Gandhiji at camp Jambusar on the 22nd instant.

We agreed there that having regard to the past history of the house and the stage we have now reached in the National struggle for freedom the most appropriate use to which it can be put is to make it the permanent headquarters of the Indian National Congress. This means that the offices of the All India Congress Committee will be permanently located in the house and parts of it not occupied by these offices will be utilised for other National purposes to be determined later in consultation with the members of the Working Committee. Meanwhile I desire to know if the Working Committee approves and accepts the main idea.

I append two short notes -one giving a brief history of the house and the site and the other a specification of the property I propose to dedicate to the Nation.

I desire to carry out the proposal on the 6th of April next which is the first day of the National Week and the day fixed by Gandhiji for the first act of concerted civil disobedience in the campaign of Independence.

In the event of my offer being accepted I should like the house to be re-named "Swaraj Bhawan"(Independence Hall).

                            Yours sincerely,

Facing page: Motilal's letter to the Congress President, dedicating his family home to the nation.

Inset: Motilal at the dedication ceremony of Swaraj Bhawan (Abode of Freedom) on 9 April 1930. Also seen are Indira and Jawaharlal.

The immediate family, c. 1929. Seated: Swarup Rani, Motilal and Kamala. Standing: Jawaharlal, Vijaya Lakshmi Pandit, Krishna Kumari, Indira and R.S Pandit.

partnership became vitally important to them both. Their interests, one leading the Swaraj Party and the other heading the Independent Party, converged in a way that made cooperation between the two mutually beneficial. Intellectually, they were on the same track. Motilal had the felicitous ability to create an atmosphere in which every participant did his best to contribute to the common task. Jinnah was alien to the wheeling-dealing tactics of various factions and therefore displayed an occasional wildness in judgement.

Jamnadas Dwarkadas records a conversation at Jinnah's house in the presence of Motilal and R.D. Tata. Jinnah kept the table roaring with laughter by recalling certain incidents in the Assembly. One of these occurred before the final voting on a particular Bill. Ratan Tata rushed to Jinnah's suite of rooms in the Cecil Hotel, complaining that a member of the Assembly asked for a big consideration to vote in favour of the Bill, and threatened that if he did not get it, he would vote against it. He belonged to Motilal's party. Jinnah at that late hour immediately sent for the member staying in the same hotel and told him, 'R.D. Tata has complained to me that you have demanded ten thousand rupees for your vote. You will not get that money. You go to hell and now you get out of this room.' Crestfallen, the member withdrew quickly and the next day he voted for the Bill. 'Ruttie, Motilal and I enjoyed this story,' Dwarkadas wrote, 'as R.D. Tata confirmed that what Jinnah had said was true and Motilal already knew all about it.'

With their record of understanding and cooperation, Motilal was confident of persuading Jinnah to accept the Nehru Report. But his expectations were belied by the intense reactions,

especially from the Ali brothers, to separate electorates and weightages for the Muslims being done away with in the Nehru Report. The claims and counter-claims led to the hardening of attitudes. After the All-Parties National Convention in December 1928, Lajpat Rai, heading the Hindu Mahasabha group, warned Motilal not to offer any concessions to Jinnah.

By the time Motilal chaired the Congress session in December 1928, the rupture between the Congress and the foremost Muslim leaders had taken place. The break between Motilal, who made dominion status the pivot of the settlement, and a section of the Congress also widened. To Jawaharlal, Bose and several others, the Nehru Report had reversed the resolution demanding complete independence adopted by the Madras Congress in 1927. Ultimately, a compromise was reached in Calcutta through Gandhi's efforts: if the British did not grant dominion status within a year the

Facing page: Motilal before imprisonment in 1930 and (below) after release in 1930. He died months after he was released on 6 February 1931. Choudhry Khaliquzzaman, who moved to Pakistan after Partition, said this about Motilal in the 1950s:

'It is sad to find that in India he is remembered as the father of Jawaharlal. What an irony! If his politics had been allowed by the Congress to be pursued without let or hindrance, India would perhaps not have been partitioned.'

Congress would launch civil disobedience to wrest complete independence.

The year (1928) Motilal chaired the Calcutta Congress was one of increased conflict between the Congress and an intransigent government. Thousands suffered as anti-Simon Commission protests flared up in city after city. Lala Lajpat Rai died after being beaten down by lathi-swinging police. The bitterness caused by the Nehru Report complicated the task of reconciling various linguistic, regional and communitarian claims. Motilal believed that, 'no amount of formulae based upon mutual concessions which those making them have no right to make will bring us nearer Hindu-Muslim unity than we are at present.'

Ansari differed. He felt that Gandhi's way of bringing about unity had already proved ineffective when conditions for joint action were ideal, and he reiterated his faith in mutual adjustments through dialogue. T.A.K. Sherwani, Khaliquzzaman and Syed Mahmud, all close to the Nehru household, agreed. Yet, civil disobedience ran its course and Ansari, once a staunch critic, stayed with it as a loyal soldier. At first, Motilal dismissed Gandhi's plans for the breach of salt laws, but, by March 1930, he supported them. In 1920, he and his family had changed their lifestyle in response to non-cooperation; in April 1930, he gifted Anand Bhawan to the Congress.

In Allahabad, the Nehrus captured the headlines with their enthusiasm. Swarup Rani was dutiful as ever. She was beaten repeatedly with heavy canes by the police and was found lying by the wayside. This incident sent a wave of horror and indignation throughout the country. 'The thought of my frail old mother lying bleeding on the dusty road obsessed me,' Jawaharlal wrote, 'and I wondered how I would have behaved if I had been there.' Kamala, who was jailed in Lucknow from 1 January to 26 January 1931, met her responsibilities with an uncomplaining stoicism, and Vijaya Lakshmi and Krishna shared the nationalist fervour. Even the twelve-year-old Indira was seen readying the children's *Vanar Sena* (children's 'army'). Motilal invested great hopes in her. She was young, intelligent and displayed signs of the rebelliousness of her father. Years later, during the

Telegram to Jawaharlal on his father's death.

Facing page: Motilal's cremation in Allahabad, 6 February 1931. 'I am going soon, Mahatmaji,' said Motilal to Gandhi on his deathbed, 'and I shall not be here to see Swaraj. But I know that you won it and will soon have it.'

Quit India movement, she and her husband Feroze Gandhi, 'a stocky, fair young man', organized an agitation in Allahabad. Both were sent to Naini Central Prison. Indira shared prison life with, among others, her aunt Vijaya Lakshmi from 11 September 1942 to 13 May 1943. The author Edward Thompson told Jawaharlal, 'You Nehrus have been very very lucky in many ways, and lucky most of all in your charming and splendid women.'

Motilal's own commitment was profoundly transparent. 'He told us,' Jawaharlal recorded in *The Discovery of India*, 'how he had been agreeably surprised to see the energy, courage and ability displayed by women all over the country; of the girls of his own household he spoke with affectionate pride.' Motilal directed the satyagraha crusade energetically before being packed off to Naini prison on 30 June 1930, and was looked after by his son: 'I wish there were many fathers to boast of such sons.'

Meanwhile, honours and distinctions were

P.N.VARMA & Co. ALLAHABAD

showered upon Motilal almost as a matter of course; these were tributes to his legal acumen and personal achievements, but also to the value of the things he stood for. Motilal was, in turn, greatly flattered by the attentions, by the confidences, and by his importance in the freedom struggle. But the strain of work, which he seemed to do with such remorseless ease, took its toll. His doctor, Ansari, had warned him of his ailments towards the end of February 1930, but he had ignored his advice. Not long after, his health broke down in Allahabad and he died on 6 February 1931.

'Man is born, he suffers, and he dies,' Nayantara Sahgal quoted Somerset Maugham to her mother Vijaya Lakshmi. 'Well, of course,' said the latter matter of factly, 'but lots of wonderful things happen to him in between.' Motilal would have nodded in approval.

Biographies end with the subject's death. The story of the Nehrus, however, has no such natural termination. If Motilal had lived until the stroke of midnight on 15 August 1947, he would have been proud of his son unfurling India's tricoloured flag. However, one person close to the family, also a Kashmiri Pandit of great distinction, had seen it all and grasped the event's significance: 'I must be prepared for the end soon. I must bless my stars that I have seen the freedom of India with you at the helm.' This was Sapru writing to Jawaharlal Nehru, free India's first Prime Minister, on 2 December 1948 with the blessing:

Tum salamat raho hazar baras
Har baras ke hon din pachas hazar.
(May you live a thousand years
May each year have fifty thousand days.)

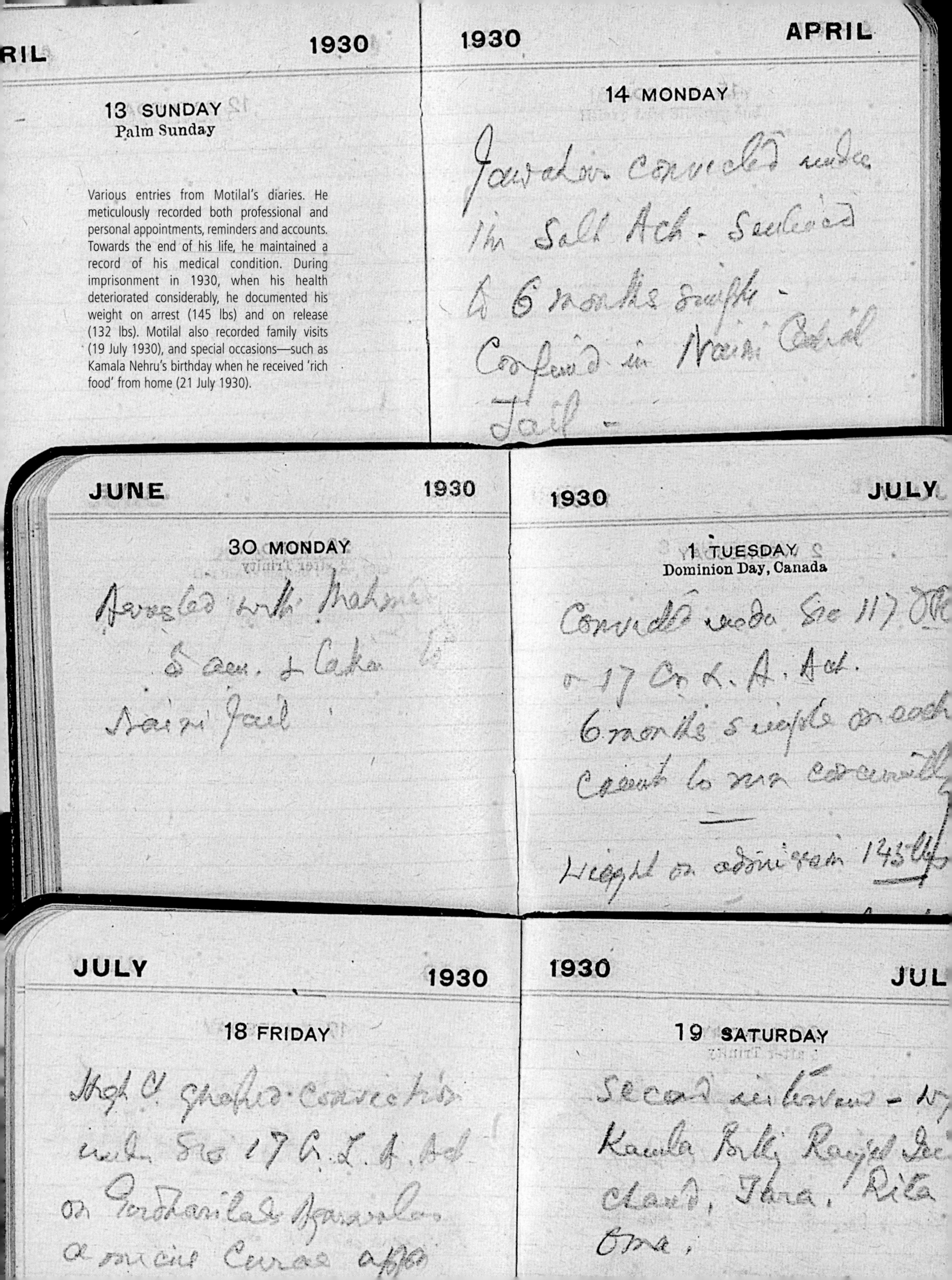

13 SUNDAY
Palm Sunday

Various entries from Motilal's diaries. He meticulously recorded both professional and personal appointments, reminders and accounts. Towards the end of his life, he maintained a record of his medical condition. During imprisonment in 1930, when his health deteriorated considerably, he documented his weight on arrest (145 lbs) and on release (132 lbs). Motilal also recorded family visits (19 July 1930), and special occasions—such as Kamala Nehru's birthday when he received 'rich food' from home (21 July 1930).

14 MONDAY

Jawahar convicted under the Salt Act. Sentenced to 6 months simple. Confined in Naini Central Jail.

30 MONDAY

Arrested with Mahmud & sen. & taken to Naini Jail

1 TUESDAY
Dominion Day, Canada

Convicted under Sec 117, 117 & 17 Cr. L. A. Act. 6 months simple on each count to run concurrently.

Weight on admission 145 lbs

18 FRIDAY

High C. graded conviction under Sec 17 C. L. A. Act on Pandit Jawaharlal a similar case aff

19 SATURDAY

Second interview. wt. Kamala, Betty, Ranjit, Indu chand, Tara, Rita, Uma.

20 SUNDAY
5 after Trinity

Smoked 48 ~~cigarettes~~ ~~in day~~

in 3 days - 16 daily.

To be reduced to 12 daily.

Began Pearl Draught 8 p.m.

21 MONDAY

Last injection of Sera - 0.73 gms

B.P. 155/96.

Sex weak reports from Sera.

Robin gave injection in own hand?

Kaula's birthday - received from home -

8 MONDAY

Suddenly Released from Naini Jail

= Calcium injection

= Consulted Hakim Md Ahsan who diagnosed blood coming from brain. took his medicine from this afternoon.

= fought out blood clots like red trees -

= weight on leaving Jail 131+1 = 132 lbs

9 TUESDAY

Hakim's treatment contd.

= Less blood in sputum

= after noon's sleep very little trace of blood.

164

JAWAHARLAL NEHRU
destiny's child

'The stars were out and shining brightly when we returned lonely and desolate.' This Jawaharlal wrote after lighting his father's funeral pyre on the banks of the Ganga. In later years, he wondered if he had repaid the love and care that had been lavished upon him by his father. 'I have had to face that question often,' he once wrote, 'and every time I have felt shame at my own record. Sometimes wider issues intervened and I was troubled and torn asunder and knew not what to do.' These 'wider issues' surfaced, first of all, over non-cooperation in 1920, and, in 1928–29, over dominion status. But he was extremely proud of his father, whose life inspired and strengthened him. 'Trying to judge him not as his son but independently of it,' he wrote to Indira before she sailed with Kamala to Switzerland in early May 1935, 'I believe he was a really great man.'

More personal tragedies followed Motilal's death. Kamala's health deteriorated because of which Jawaharlal was let out for eleven days in August 1934. She died on 28 February 1936; her ashes were poured into the bosom of the swift-flowing Ganga. 'How many of our forbears,' Jawaharlal remarked, 'she [Ganga] had carried thus to the sea, how many of those who follow us will take that last journey in the embrace of her water.' He dedicated his *Autobiography* 'To Kamala, who is no more.' Then, his mother passed away in January 1938.

These bereavements shattered Jawaharlal's confidence. He was to write in the Ahmadnagar Fort Prison in April 1944: 'The old exuberance is much less now, the almost uncontrollable impulses have toned down, and passions and feeling are more in check.' Yet his energy and commitments sustained him. For one, he withstood the criticism of the left by spelling out his social and economic ideas with a little more clarity than before. After visiting Russia in 1927, he had been convinced that the solution of India's poverty and rural backwardness lay in adopting modern industrial techniques rather than hand spinning and hand weaving. Contrary to Gandhi's ideas that ranged from charkha to trusteeship, he ardently championed socialism from the Congress platform as its President in 1929 and 1936. India, he said, would have to adopt a full socialistic programme if it was to end poverty and inequality. At the same time, he felt uneasy with leftist groups, who spent much of their energy in mutual conflicts and recriminations over finer points of doctrine. 'Life is too complicated,' he observed, 'and, as far as we can understand it in our present

Facing page: 'We can make no complaints that life has treated us harshly, for ours has been a willing choice, and perhaps life has not been so bad to us after all. For only they can sense life who stand often on the verge of it, only they whose lives are not governed by the fear of death. In spite of all the mistakes that we may have made, we have saved ourselves from triviality and an inner shame and cowardice. That, for our individual selves, has been some achievement.'
—Jawaharlal Nehru, *The Discovery of India*

state of knowledge, too illogical, for it to be confined within the four corners of a fixed doctrine'.

During the election battle that ultimately brought the Congress ministries to power in 1937, he discussed some of these ideas, including his explicit denunciation of imperialism. He noticed the people's extraordinary enthusiasm during a frenetic 130-day tour in 1937. As he moved about, he found himself addressing as many as a dozen meetings with upwards of a hundred thousand people a day, and at the end reckoned he had addressed something like 10 million people all told. In his *Autobiography* (1957), Rajendra Prasad recalled: 'I do not think that any Congress President (Jawaharlal had chaired the Faizpur Congress session in 1936) had ever strained himself to that extent and done so much to awaken the masses.' Ultimately, his energy and commitment paid off. The Congress won overall majorities in the provincial elections in five of the eleven provinces of India. An elated Jawaharlal told Stafford Cripps, who was sent to India in the spring of 1942 to offer independence after the war was over:

> As a whole India is wide awake and expectant … My extensive touring has been a revelation to me of the suppressed energy of the people and of their passionate desire to be rid of their burdens. The Congress is supreme today so far as the masses and the lower middle classes are concerned. It has hardly ever been in such a position.

Jawaharlal contributed to this awakening because, next to Gandhi, he was India's most popular leader. In October 1935, Ansari had said that Jawaharlal was undoubtedly the idol of the people, and that 'his place in the hearts of the people and of Congress is ensured forever.' To retain that place, he worked tirelessly, trying to persuade the Congress ministers, who had tasted power in 1937, to fulfill the Congress goals. In many places, his efforts yielded tangible results. In others, the people's expectations remained unfulfilled. In Bihar and UP, the ministries pursued pro-landlord policies. In Bombay, the Industrial Disputes Bill (1938) triggered a major strike that caused anger, disappointment and frustration. Their attitude towards the labour movement, wrote Jayaprakash Narayan angrily, 'should be an eye-opener to those who do not wish that the Ministries should be utilized to bind the workers' organization hand and foot and deliver them to the employers'.

A singularly important outcome of Jawaharlal's endeavours was the Muslim Mass Contact Campaign. According to him, the Congress had for too long thought in terms of pacts and compromises with communal leaders, and neglected the people behind them. He called it a 'discredited policy'. While campaigning, he struck a favourable chord with the Muslims and wished to take advantage of their 'new interest and awakening'. By impressing on poor villagers that they would be better off under a Congress dispensation, he wanted to wean them away from the Muslim League and draw them into the nationalist fold.

On 31 March 1937, he directed Congress committees to concentrate on enrolling Muslims, and suggested the formation of committees to take in hand the work of increasing contacts with the Muslim masses living in rural and urban areas. The All India Congress Committee (AICC) set up a cell to control and direct activities relating to Muslims, to propagate the Congress programme, and to counteract anti-Congress propaganda. Kunwar Mohammad Ashraf, one of Jawaharlal's most trusted lieutenants, received charge of the cell.

But this initiative ran into rough weather. Apprehending that the triumph of mass contact would bolster Jawaharlal's image and provide him, as in the case of Gandhi during the Khilafat days, with a solid base among Muslims, right-wing Congress leaders girded themselves to resist it. Thus G.B. Pant, Chief Minister of UP, advised Jawaharlal that the Congress should stick to its old policy and creed of representing the Indian masses regardless of caste or creed. People like him recalled the Khilafat and non-cooperation days when the Mahatma pandered to the religious sentiments of the Muslims and allowed them to dictate Congress policies. Now, they faced the cheerless prospect of yet another Muslim 'influx'. Fearful that the Muslims would wrest major concessions and influence Congress policies, they spared no effort to sabotage mass contact.

Doubtless, Jawaharlal and other protagonists of mass contact confronted numerous difficulties: Jinnah's stout resistance, lukewarm support of party comrades, and communal animosities manifest in Hindu-Muslim rioting and other forms of antagonism. These problems were not insurmountable, however, as would appear from Jawaharlal's own assessment of the communal situation. The League was, after all, weak, divided, and disorganized, and its leader, Jinnah, did not yet command the allegiance of the more powerful groups in Punjab, UP, and Bengal. The Congress, however, enjoyed a fair measure of support, a fact that places Jinnah's outburst against mass contact and the League's endeavours to arrest its progress,

in perspective. The Congress' inability to consolidate the gains of 1937–38 was a sure case of letting an opportunity slip by. By letting the mass contact campaign peter out, the Congress created spaces for Jinnah to take advantage of the outbreak of war and the deteriorating communal relations and to rally his community around the symbol of a separate Muslim homeland.

On 14 November 1939, Jawaharlal turned fifty. He had progressed, stated Mahadev Desai, Gandhi's personal secretary, 'geometrically rather than arithmetically'. Gandhi, then in Sevagram (Wardha), hoped that he would complete the other half 'retaining the same vigour, frankness and robust humanity'. Jawaharlal felt old, tired, mentally weary, and 'something apart from the world I live in'. He added: 'Life is a curious affair and puzzles and perplexes me far more than it used to do when I was younger and had more assurance. That assurance fades out. What do I know, what do I understand?'

For the Nehrus, there was no time to celebrate. In September 1939, the war clouds had broken out. And when the Viceroy simply declared India to be at war after Britain's own declaration of war on Germany, the Congress demanded both an immediate definition of war aims and an immediate declaration of independence. The provincial ministries resigned. Beatrice Webb, whom Jawaharlal admired, wrote in her diary on 5 October 1939, 'Nehru has called the British bluff, the pretence of fighting for political democracy and rights of man.' The fact is that he did not want to take advantage of Britain's distress. He said: '*Yeh baat Hindustan ki shaan ke khilaaf hae, ke woh England kee kamzoree se faida uthaa kar iss waqt Satyaghraha shuroo kar dey'*. (It is against India's dignity to take advantage of England's weakness and launch satyagraha.) Many tall leaders in the Congress leadership disagreed. Azad was one of them. 'We cannot grope in the dark,' he told Jawaharlal, 'like blind men. We should adopt a way with open eyes.'

On this occasion too, Gandhi's differences with Jawaharlal came to the fore, and he urged him to be patient. 'I know,' Gandhi wrote on 24 October 1940, 'what strain you are bearing in giving me your loyalty. I prize it beyond measure.' Having spurned the Viceroy's initiatives, Gandhi had launched civil disobedience from the autumn of 1940. Vinoba Bhave inaugurated, on 17 October, the individual satyagraha movement by delivering an anti-war speech at Paunar, a village near Wardha. Jawaharlal was arrested on 31 October at Chheoki railway station while returning from Wardha. Subsequently, he was sentenced to four years' imprisonment. He passed most of this prison sentence back in his old 'home', the jail at Dehra Dun.

In mid-November, the campaign's second phase began with the arrests of the Congress Working Committee (CWC) and AICC members, and of the Congress representatives in the central and provincial legislatures. The third phase, opened in January 1941, was renewed in April. It was marked by a sharp increase in the number of satyagrahis. In the meantime, Gandhi had planned his move with meticulous care, and lifted the struggle to a high moral plane, above the entanglements and local factions and priorities that had dogged the Congress as a party in power.

Jawaharlal's release on 4 December 1941, along with other political prisoners who had courted imprisonment, did not lead to any significant reappraisal of his stand—that India would join the War only if Britain granted assurance for its constitutional advance. His negotiations with Cripps, who arrived in India on 22 March 1942, failed. This led him to endorse Gandhi's plan of giving the British an ultimatum to quit India. On 8 August, he moved and Patel seconded the 'quit India' resolution at the AICC meeting. Earlier, on 27 July, he informed the peasants in Allahabad of an impending mass movement in the country. In other speeches he made it clear that there was no question of Congressmen deliberately choosing to go to jail, that the Congress might perish in the terrible ordeal ahead of it, but that a free India would emerge out of its ashes.

On 9 August, the CWC members were arrested in Bombay. Gandhi landed up in the Aga Khan's palace, and Jawaharlal in the Ahmadnagar fort to begin his sentence of 1,041 days. Sitting in Ahmadnagar Fort as 'a prisoner perforce inactive when a fierce activity consumes the world', Jawaharlal fretted a little and thought of 'the big things and brave ventures' that had filled his mind. The only solace was that he could read, write and look at the world in the face, as Gandhi had suggested on that fateful evening of 8 August 1942, 'with calm and clear eyes even though the eyes of the world are blood-shot today'.

❧

The twenty-first month of my imprisonment is well on its way; the moon waxes and wanes and soon two years will have been completed. Another birthday will come round to remind me that I am getting older; my last four birthdays I have spent in prison, here [Ahmadnagar Fort Prison] and in Dehra Dun Jail, and many others in the course of my previous terms of imprisonment. I have lost count of their number.

— *The Discovery of India*

The most vivid part of Jawaharlal's existence was lived quite apart from the family, while the part of his life spent in the company of friends was in jail. Quoting Auguste Comte, he noted in *The Discovery of India,* 'We live dead men's lives, encased in our pasts, but this is especially so in prison where we try to find some sustenance for our starved and locked-up emotions in memory of the past or fancies of the future.' To Indira, he wrote on 16 April 1943, 'Prison is the true home of that dreadful thing ennui, and yet, oddly enough, it teaches us to triumph over it.'

During those years, spread as they were across an agonizingly long period, Jawaharlal continued to write with his usual prodigality. The superimposed loneliness, commented Halide Edib, gave him 'the power to turn to himself for fellowship and guidance, and arrange his thoughts and evolve his political creed undisturbed by external influences'. He did not have the time to access his library in Anand Bhawan, but the accumulated mass of notes, to which he kept making additions, became the main source of his writings.

Even though he cast his net wide, the breadth of view and the patient learning revealed in *Glimpses of World History*, *An Autobiography* and *The Discovery of India* is indeed astonishing. These books reflect the changes in his interests that had taken place in his public life, his heightened concerns with social affairs, with politics, and with the liberation struggles in India and overseas. His other writings were, in their own ways, solid achievements. They reflect an attitude to science and religion, an attitude that accounts for the immense popularity of his works, particularly among the young. In old age, Bertrand Russell, whom Jawaharlal admired, took to writing fiction, which was, he says in his *Autobiography*, 'a great release of my hitherto unexpressed feelings'. Jawaharlal's *An Autobiography*, probably the most revealing thing he ever wrote, did just that. It came in 1936, offering readers an objective scrutiny and analysis both of self and of events. The writer Rafiq Zakaria, then in school, read it from cover to cover. 'There was something so moving about the narration of the story,' he wrote later, 'of our hopes and aspirations in its pages that no Indian who read it could escape its magical effects. There was something so regal about the personality of the author who emerged out of its pages with such power and grace that the spell it cast was overwhelming. It drew the readers to the author as a duck to the water.'

'Prison is not a pleasant place to live in even for a short period, much less for long years. But it was a privilege for me to live in close contact with men of outstanding ability and culture and a wide human outlook which even the passions of the moment did not obscure,' wrote Jawaharlal in *The Discovery of India*. Khan Abdul Ghaffar Khan was one such person. He was deeply attached to him, an attachment that once took the form of a dream. Jawaharlal wrote how, in the heat of a summer afternoon, he dozed off. In his dream, he saw the 'Frontier Gandhi' being attacked and he fighting to defend him. He woke up in an exhausted state 'feeling very miserable'. He added: 'That surprised me, for in my waking state I was not liable to such emotional outbursts.'

Jawaharlal's other favourite was Abul Kalam Azad, 'an extraordinarily interesting companion', whom he knew for over two decades. Full of learning and wise in counsel, he described him as 'a finished product of the culture that, in these disturbed days, unhappily pertains to few…' At the same time, he found him to be out of place in the modern world. That is because his perspective was political and not social or economic. His astonishing memory and encyclopedic knowledge were impressive, but Jawaharlal could not understand why so learned a person wrote so little. The fact is that the Maulana was as discursive as a medieval romancer and as fond of the colourful as a medieval chronicler.

These impressions stayed, though the post-1942 years strained their bonding. Outwardly, they were comrades-in-arms, but Azad seemed, at least retrospectively, uneasy with the entire process of the transfer of power. He argued—a view that seems untenable today—that Jawaharlal could have averted the cataclysmic event and avoided the bloodshed and strife in the aftermath of Independence.

～

Nakarda gunahon ki bhi hasrat ki mile dad
Ya rab agar in karda gunahon ki saza hai
(If we are to be punished for the sins we have committed, at least we should be praised for not yearning for the sins we have not committed).

This is one of Mirza Ghalib's verses that Jawaharlal quoted to his daughter, who he lovingly called Indu, in a letter from jail. By the time he and other members of the CWC were set free on 14 June

1945, the great Bengal Famine had claimed 3 million victims. Moreover, the recurrence of Hindu-Muslim violence had exposed the fragility of inter-community peace. And the Muslim League had acquired salience in Indian politics that gave Jinnah the assured status of representing his community's sole voice. Aided first by Linlithgow and later by his successor, Wavell, he moved from strength to strength. In the end, he earned his Pakistan.

Jawaharlal's perspective on the 'communal problem' was influenced by his upbringing in Allahabad, his interactions with the Urdu-speaking elite of the Indo-Gangetic belt, and his exposure to the Fabian socialists in Cambridge and London. His understanding was also enriched by exchanges with Muslim scholars who introduced him to Indian Islam and medieval Indian history. He could therefore analyze late nineteenth-century reformist currents, appreciate Syed Ahmad Khan's bold initiatives, and grasp the significance of the impact of Azad and Iqbal on the younger generation of Muslims. It is important to stress here the advantage which his freedom and freshness of outlook gave him and the astonishing insight and energy which enabled him to see the significance of these men in the history of Indian Islam.

He attributed the social, educational and economic backwardness of most Muslims not to any innate failing but to concrete historical and sociological factors. In fact, the Muslims he met or addressed did not ask him about percentages or separate electorates, but about land revenue or rent, debt, water rates, unemployment, and their many other burdens. How could he, then, accept the League's pretentious claims, and recognize Jinnah as the 'sole spokesman' of the Muslims? In his opinion, the League leaders wanted to prevent radical changes not because of a Hindu majority but because of the fear that the Congress would do away with semi-feudal privileges. Even though they deliberately exploited religion in order to avoid discussing the common man's problems, the real conflict 'was essentially between those who stood for a nationalist/democratic/socially revolutionary policy and those concerned with preserving the relics of a feudal regime'. His remedy was to 'scotch our so-called religion', secularize the intelligentsia, and encourage adult franchise that would make people think more along economic lines.

Jawaharlal believed in fortifying traditional linkages between different communities through mass contact and a radical socio-economic programme, and wanted the Congress to make the people aware of their mutual interdependence, their shared experiences, and their common concerns, interests and destiny. He asked: Why were the interests of the Muslim peasant different from those of the Hindu peasant, or those of a Muslim labourer, artisan, merchant, landlord or manufacturer different from those of his Hindu counterparts? They were not. Resting his optimism on this formulation, he concluded that 'the communal question will automatically be solved' once the people were drawn into the fight for freedom. Speaking at Amritsar on 31 May 1936, he reiterated that 'the day on which India achieves her freedom, communal differences and jealousies will get solved of themselves.'

Jawaharlal corresponded with Jinnah on these lines, questioned the rationale behind Muslim nationalism, and dismissed the idea of an exclusive Muslim identity. He expected him to draw his constituency into the just and legitimate struggle against the government, for he saw no solution of the Hindu-Muslim problem without the removal of the 'third party'. Jinnah disagreed, arguing that there would be no political progress till the Congress accepted his conditions. Aided by a combination of fortuitous circumstances, he managed to translate the two-nation theory into a reality. Various attempts to wean him away from his position failed. The Simla Conference in June 1945, like the one a year earlier, failed because Jinnah regarded the presence of Azad and Ghaffar Khan as a gratuitous and deliberate provocation. By the end of June 1946, the Cabinet Mission plan—it proposed a complex, three-tiered governmental scheme that involved provincial grouping—floundered. Jawaharlal rejected the groupings of Muslim majority areas therein; the Muslim league accused him of repudiating the spirit of the three-tiered federation plan. To demonstrate the strength of his support, Jinnah called for a Direct Action Day on 16 August. In Calcutta alone there were 20,000 casualties of the Hindu-Muslim riots. 'Horror has piled on horror during these past two days and I feel quite numbed,' Nehru wrote from Patna on 5 November 1946.

Wavell, the Viceroy, put together an interim government in September, but the League stayed out. When it joined the interim government a month later, the two sets of ministers were at odds with each other. With the spurt in Hindu-Muslim violence, the parting of ways was the only solution to an intractable problem. Jawaharlal told Michael Brecher, the political scientist, in the 1950s, that he and his colleagues were tired men and getting on in years. He mentioned that they could not stand the prospect of going to prison again, and if they had stood out for a united India as they wished, prison obviously awaited them. They saw the fires burning in Punjab and heard of the killings. The Partition plan offered a way out and they took it.

So ended the last prospects of a united India. Jawaharlal accepted this reality within a month of Mountbatten's arrival in India on 22 March 1947. Even though Partition painfully negated a lifetime's effort, he told Azad that it was unavoidable and that it would not be wise to oppose it. So, India's 'vivisection', an expression Gandhi used in agony and despair, occurred on 14–15 August. While Karachi celebrated, Delhi was, by contrast, in the 'dark, brooding, pock-marked with refugees, immobile with shock' (Nayantara Sahgal).

If one were to slice the 1940s as an era and view the cross-section of layers, we would view Partition under the icing of Independence. In fact, no other country in the twentieth century offers two such contrary movements in simultaneous layering. If one was a popular nationalist movement, unique in the annals of world history for ousting the colonizers through non-violent means, the other, in its underbelly, was the counter movement of Partition, marked by violence, cruelty, bloodshed, displacement and massacres. If one was a cause for celebration, the other caused deep anguish, anger and indignation. If one was an assertion of the nation's independence and sovereignty, the other was, in the same breath, the tearing asunder of the subcontinent on religious lines. It is the bizarre and horrific simultaneity of these two layerings which the fictional and non-fictional accounts capture so vividly. More than historical accounts of Independence and Partition, personal histories of uprooting speak volumes of the betrayal of the noble ideals of Indian nationalism, secularism, non-violence, and of a truly democratic state.

In conclusion, it is worth sharing the reminiscences of A.E Benthall, an Englishman who was the vice-president of the Bengal Chamber of Commerce:

SCENE I

In the autumn of 1947 Gandhi arrived in Calcutta and stayed in a tumble-down house on the outskirts of Calcutta, near one of the scenes of the worst Hindu-Muslim riots. Soon, he realized that one of the principal causes of the rioting was the terrible condition under which hundreds of thousands of people lived. They had no roof over their heads at all, and millions lived in slums. He therefore summoned leading businessmen of all descriptions in order to rebuild Calcutta. He wanted the project to be completed within two years.

Benthall set off to the rendezvous, but on the way encountered a riot. Bombs were exploding and guns were being fired, and the streets were littered with glass and stones, he wrote. When he reached the house, he found Gandhi sitting on a low wooden platform, spinning, and wearing only a loincloth. A small girl sat on the platform near him, apparently learning to spin, or perhaps ministering to his needs.

Twenty minutes after the meeting, a mob of young Hindus broke into the house. They were furious because the Mahatma's influence had prevented them from organizing a general massacre of Muslims in Calcutta. They demanded that he should immediately withdraw his opposition and if he did not, they would kill him. The Mahatma did not stop spinning. One of the young men then aimed a blow at his head with a lathi. The little girl sitting beside him caught the blow on her arm. Gandhi continued to spin.

Nobody else in the crowd then had the courage to strike the Mahatma again. They merely vented their fury on the building, pulled the window frames out of the walls, smashed the doors, and reduced the scanty furniture to matchwood. And yet, from the moment when the little girl saved the Mahatma's life, the rioting in Calcutta ceased, and nothing of the sort occurred in the city for a good many months.

SCENE II

From 1947 to 1950 Benthall had a number of meetings with Jawaharlal, sometimes in company with others, and sometimes alone. He recalled his visit to Calcutta, soon after Independence, to combat the rioting and massacres that were taking place in Bengal. The Prime Minister sat at a desk that had on it a large inkpot, some pens and pencils, and the weighty volume of Thacker's *Indian Directory*.

A discussion took place about how best to combat the communal ill feeling. It proceeded on sensible lines for some time, but after a bit some Marwaris made an impassioned appeal for the Indian Army to go into East Pakistan to rescue the Hindus, who, it was alleged, were being massacred there.

Jawaharlal listened for a short time, but then suddenly appeared to lose his temper. He picked up the directory, raised it to the full length of his arms above his head, and brought it smashing down on the desk. This action he repeated three or four times, with greater and greater force. The inkpot, pens, etc., scattered on to the floor. He accused the Marwaris of deliberately planning a war and a massacre of Muslims, though they themselves were prevented by their Jain religion from taking up arms

or even crushing a mosquito. He continued with extraordinary eloquence until the Marwaris slunk out of the room, leaving only people from other communities to listen to the Prime Minister. Shortly after that the meeting dispersed.

In fact, added Benthall to his description, no Hindus were massacred in East Bengal at that time, though hundreds of thousands were driven out to take refuge in West Bengal. Nehru was of course right in refusing to send the army across the new frontier, and his violent reaction to such a suggestion was typical of the man.

⤳

Jawaharlal had reflected in *The Discovery of India* that a dream of unity had occupied the mind of India since the dawn of civilization. Liberation from colonial rule was the first tangible step towards its realization. India was free at the stroke of midnight, and its tryst with destiny began with the Prime Minister's memorable speech. He stated:

> Long years ago we made a tryst with destiny, and now the time comes when we shall redeem our pledge, not wholly or in full measure, but very substantially. At the stroke of the midnight hour, when the world sleeps, India will awake to life and freedom. A moment comes, which comes but rarely in history, when we step out from the old to the new, when an age ends, and when the soul of a nation, long suppressed, finds utterance. It is fitting that at this solemn moment we take the pledge of dedication to the service of India and her people and to the still larger cause of humanity.

The journey towards peace, progress and prosperity began haltingly. First, tribesmen entered the

Kashmir valley from Pakistan and marched on Srinagar. With India and Pakistan on the brink of war, the United Nations intervened, and on 1 January 1949, a truce line was established which left two-thirds of Kashmir in India's hands and one-third with Pakistan. (Jawaharlal wrestled in vain with the Kashmir issue until his death. Often, he played into the hands of advisors against his own better judgement. A case in point was the arrest of Shaikh Abdullah, his close friend and admirer who shared with him the ideal of a secular state in which Hindus and Muslims could live peaceably. This was a monumental folly. Equally, the choice of leaders to replace Abdullah made very little sense. Most of them turned out to be notoriously corrupt, inept, and repressive.)

Meanwhile, there was no let-up in Partition violence. Everything for which Gandhi and Jawaharlal had spent their lives fighting crumbled before their eyes. But free India's first Prime Minister was not one to yield to these fissiparous tendencies or make concessions to the communalists. In the capital itself he himself took personal risks trying to shame the rioters into submission. There are other examples of his intervening in cases where he felt that justice had not been done. Thus he commented on the draconian evacuee property laws that deprived Muslims from getting back their properties after Partition, and the unauthorized occupation of *waqf* properties and mosques. In the case of Roshan Ara, a young girl who lost her family during the riots, Jawaharlal's intervention made her rehabilitation possible.

National reconciliation was the cornerstone of Jawaharlal's nation-building strategy. Consequently, he exhorted his audience to eschew casteism and communalism, to abhor sectarian violence, to strive for achieving higher goals, and to share a common destiny. But his worldview did not appeal to all. A major disaster struck India at 5 p.m. on 30 January 1948, when a Hindu fanatic sprang out of the Friday congregation and shot the father of the nation four times at point blank range. 'The light has gone out,' a traumatized Prime Minister informed the nation. He told the Constituent Assembly that 'a glory has departed and the sun that warmed and brightened our lives has set and we shiver in the cold and dark.'

Meanwhile, the Constituent Assembly debates offered a way out of the nation's dilemmas and predicaments. With an abundant faith in the common man and the ultimate success of democratic rule, its members sought to break down the provincialism of local loyalties through direct election by adult suffrage. To many, these urges and the initial moves towards their fulfillment captured the spirit and essence of nationalism. Democracy bestowed an aura of legitimacy on modern political life: laws, rules and policies appeared justified when they were democratic. Leaders differed in intellectual outlook and leadership style, and yet they shared a single vision of the system of rule to guide the new nation. It was a parliamentary system, its leaders answerable to the people through elections.

During the deliberations from 1946 to 1949, ending with the proclamation of the Republic on 26 January 1950, Jawaharlal shone like a bright light, marshalling his inexhaustible resources from the floor to make a strong case for building an egalitarian social order. He stated that the Constituent Assembly's first task was to give free India a liberal constitution. In fact, he settled the general lines on which the Constitution was to be drawn up. He had drafted and moved the Objectives Resolution in December 1946, stipulating that India would be an independent sovereign republic. Later, he ensured that the Congress created a parliamentary democracy and that English remained one of the official languages until at least 1965. A protagonist of social justice, equity, minority rights, and a scientific temper, he also defended powerfully not only the principle of separating religion from politics but also a *secular* constitution. To him, the idea of two nations, each based on a religion, went against the secularity on which the Indian state was established.

⌒

…We have to judge how the mind and heart of India functions. Are the people strong and stable or get easily carried away? Are we led astray by a momentary passion or do we take action calmly and after a careful judgement even when there is danger of something that we do not like? There is a difference between individuals or nations which get carried away and those who remain calm and strong in a crisis, whether it is war or something else.

This is India's first Prime Minister speaking at Delhi's sprawling Ramlila Grounds on 23 September 1956. In the context of the country's democratic journey, this speech reveals the importance he attached to an open-ended dialogue with the people. In fact, his greatest fulfillment came while facing or addressing a crowd. Nayantara Sahgal, who travelled with him on a number of occasions, describes 'the huge brown blur that assembled wherever he spoke, the men and women who lined the roads when his car drove past, the people he did not know by name but whose needs washed up against him in daily work were his sustenance'. Contact with them 'transcended fatigue and discouragement, kindled a lambent optimism'.

The same spirit, of sharing, advice and consultation, is reflected in the exchanges with chief ministers. He kept them posted not only on party affairs but also on complex arguments on, for example, capitalism and socialism. 'I am sorry to inflict these theoretical arguments upon you,' he once wrote to them. We do not know how the Chief Ministers responded, but they knew full well that the Prime Minister had set a healthy tradition of engagement with them.

Two incidents illustrate Jawaharlal's open-minded nature and liberal outlook. One relates to the opposition by some people in 1956 to the inclusion of two distinguished writers on the Sahitya Akademi's Advisory Board because of their pro-communist proclivities. Jawaharlal overruled them. Again, when some people showed reluctance in screening *Pather Panchali* at London's National Theatre because of Satyajit Ray's portrayal of poverty, he told the concerned Minister: 'I do not agree with this viewpoint. We are a poor county and we should not be ashamed of it, except that we should get rid of poverty.'

At the risk of oversimplification, it must be said that, unlike neighbouring Pakistan, India's national movement bequeathed a set of leaders who were better equipped to cope with such controversies. Jawaharlal's vision, combined with his pragmatic approach, made all the difference. In 1940, Subhas Chandra Bose had remarked that Jawaharlal would make a good Prime Minister in normal times but fail in a crisis-ridden situation. The fact is that his finest hour was after Partition. At that juncture, any other leader could have been overwhelmed by the eruption of large-scale violence and the plight of Hindu and Sikh refugees. But Jawaharlal kept his cool and led a truncated and crisis-ridden nation with great aplomb. 'For all of us in India,' he told the Chief Ministers in May 1950, 'the issue of communal unity and a secular state must be made perfectly clear. We have played about with this idea sufficiently long and moved away from it far enough. We must go back and go back not secretly or apologetically, but openly and rather aggressively.' He did not waver in his belief that religious strife must be fought tooth and nail no matter what the cost or how daunting the opposition.

To preserve national unity, he backed the States Reorganization Bill, 'an extraordinary culmination of the fierce and angry debates and all the upheavals and riots that had taken place during the past many months'. He did much to soothe tempers, even though some of his own colleagues attacked him bitterly and C.D. Deshmukh, his Finance Minister, resigned from the Cabinet. The fact is that the reorganization of states in 1956 along linguistic lines was a masterstroke: without it, India's cultural and linguistic unity could have been under threat. By agreeing to create linguistic states, the Prime Minister provided 'a vernacular political milieu' that led to the flowering of many linguistically rooted cultures and thereby evolved a system which greatly enriched India's cultural life.

Jawaharlal's principal asset was his ability to grasp the challenges faced by the postcolonial societies. He envisioned a classless society based on cooperative effort with opportunities for all, and achievable through democratic planning.

He spoke of India's approach as 'a third way which takes the best from all existing systems—the Russian, the American and others—and seeks to create something suited to one's own history and philosophy'. He assured the Congress camp on 7 October 1956 'that two or three more Five Year Plans will entirely change the face of this country'. That was wishful thinking. He knew the difficulties, as also the pitfalls, in implementing certain ideas, but he insisted that planning was the panacea of all economic ills and the road to socialism.

What was socialism? It meant uplifting people and giving them equal opportunities. It did not mean making everybody poor; it meant making people better off. He wanted everybody to know this. Jawaharlal did not expect Congressmen to be economists or specialists, but he did expect them to understand 'where we are today, where we want to go, and the main path which will lead us to our goal'. He reminded Chief Ministers that the Congress and Parliament had adopted the socialist pattern of society—'a natural development of our thinking and our national movement'—not as some rigid doctrinaire theory, but rather as a broad objective that had to be adapted to India's needs. His own views on socialism differed sharply from some of the tall leaders of the socialist group who had, for their own personal and ideological reasons, drifted away from the Congress.

His polemical exchanges with Bose in March–April 1939 show that he did not see any contradiction between being a socialist and an individualist. He said: 'I suppose I am temperamentally and by training an individualist, and intellectually a socialist. ... I hope that socialism does not kill or suppress individuality; indeed I am attracted to it because it will release innumerable individuals from economic and cultural bondage.'

The Hindu Code Bill and the Hindu Succession Act reflected Jawaharlal's reformist agenda, though he did not express the same zeal in reforming the Muslim Personal Law or enacting, in the light of the Directive Principles of State Policy, a uniform civil code. The Hindu Succession Act gave, for the first time, a share of father's property to a daughter and gave women absolute rights over self-acquired property.

These concerns went hand-in-hand with Jawaharlal's attempts to resolve the Kashmir issue and to end the stand-off with the Nagas. He desired a long-term political approach to settling the Naga issue without disturbing their traditions and customs. He justified military intervention only because some Naga leaders had turned violent. Still, he wanted the Army to make friends with them— 'our fellow citizens and not enemies' and win them over. In general, he sought to reconcile the diverse interests of various regions within the national frame, assigning, as he stated in his tribute to B.G. Tilak on 23 July 1956, a critical role to the leadership: 'It is the job of a leader not merely to reflect the people's aspiration and say what they want to hear but to learn to recognize their thoughts and emotions and to take them forward on the road to achieving their goals by giving them courage and hope.'

The combination of ideas and their implementation produced some good results; in the opinion of the educationist, K.G. Saiyidain, Jawaharlal performed 'scores of miracles, achieving so much that seemed impossible, smoothing out the strings of many a situation that seemed hopelessly entangled'. But his courage and faith could not put an end to the growing discontent with the Congress regime. Indira Gandhi reminded her father, on 17 December 1949, of 'the giant wave of unpopularity that is inundating the Congress and the Provincial Governments'. He himself felt that the party's energies were concentrated on disruptive activities.

Having spurned the Mahatma's plea to wind up their organization after Independence, many Congress leaders, fired with dreams of achieving office, were embroiled in intrigue and factionalism to grab the levers of power. The Prime Minister could neither thwart their ambitions nor curb their troublemaking instincts. He could simply bemoan, as he did just two years after Independence, that the Congress was 'simply fading away before our eyes'. In 1952, Mira Behn, one of Gandhi's disciples, echoed similar sentiments, stating that the Congress should recognize that it was the ideals that conquered, and it was those ideals alone that could successfully overcome the dangers surrounding India on all sides. Jawaharlal agreed, but he was too busy steadying and steering the Indian ship through the rough currents of Indian politics. 'Would you say,' Martin Luther King asked Jawaharlal, 'that young Indians remember the teachings of Gandhi?' He rather sadly replied that he 'thought not'.

Jawaharlal could not stem the rot and, by the time the Kamaraj Plan came to be implemented in August 1963, most observers found the Congress organization to be in disarray. His own position had become extremely vulnerable owing to the mounting opposition to his policies and the desertion of his friends who had broken ranks with him over the war with China. There were promises to keep, but time was running out. The storm of opposition was brewing only to cut Jawaharlal adrift from his people and the party.

৵

It is noteworthy that some of the key figures in India's national movement were not just concerned with the country's independence but with freedom struggles all over the world. During the inter-War years, in particular, home and international affairs were closely intertwined. The Spanish Civil War—a battle between fascism and democracy in Europe—received the attention of the Congress. Jawaharlal stated on 23 June 1938 that Gandhi and the Congress favoured a Republican Spain. At the Tripuri session in early March 1939, the Congress disapproved of British foreign policy culminating in the recognition of the Spanish government. The gates of Madrid became the symbols of human liberty; Jawaharlal organized funds to send food grains and an ambulance unit.

His initial interest in international affairs, kindled as early as 1927, developed in the 1950s around two vital issues—decolonization and disarmament. To him, both these issues had moral and pragmatic components to them. Thus, he campaigned for the abolition of nuclear weaponry—'these frightful engines of destruction'—because the emergent arms race between the superpowers was to have devastating consequences not only for the newly decolonized countries in general but for India in particular. In short, his crusade for decolonization and disarmament and his articulation of an explicit vision for foreign policy enhanced India's stature worldwide.

Jawaharlal is accused of adopting double standards on the Soviet Union's invasion of Hungary in 1956. In one of his many exchanges with the attractive but quixotic figure of Krishna Menon, he stated on 11 November 1956: 'There is much feeling in All India Congress Committee circles that our attitude in regard to Hungary has not been clear as it might have been. There is naturally great sympathy for Hungarian people and resentment at the use of Russian army in strength to suppress them.' In some of his correspondence with world leaders, he clarified India's stance on the Soviet invasion. Even though they did not heed his clarifications, they honoured his broad commitment to peace and opposition to military pacts and alliances.

On the Suez Canal, Jawaharlal declared it to be an integral part of Egypt. According to him, the real issue was oil and not the contest over the Suez Canal. That indeed was so. The end result of Great Britain's belligerence led to India's involvement in some of the negotiations over the Suez affair. He not only acted in unison with the other main players in the non-aligned movement, but also positioned his country as a key player in world affairs.

In 1956, Jawaharlal had stated:

It is my job to understand the present situation in the world and even to voice India's opinion on one side or the other side. Therefore, my mind is full of the complexities of the world, the international situation and preparations of war. I am perturbed because where will all these military preparations lead the world to? Will it go up in flames?

Speaking philosophically, he observed:

I do not know what is ultimately the right way. Perhaps, there are many ways and each individual has to seek his way to do good or to counter evil. But whatever ways there may be surely the way of violence is not a good heir. Surely, the way of hatred is not a good way, and I think we can say this with some assurance. And not only because in principle and in theory it is not good but also because of the evidence of our eyes, the evidence of our history, the evidence of recent events has shown that the way of violence is not even a practical way, apart from theory and apart from idealism.

∽

Ranj se khugar hua insan to mit jata hai ranj
Mushkilain itni pari mujh par ke asaan ho gain
(When a person becomes accustomed to grief then grief is erased. So many difficulties fell upon me that they became easy)

The story of Jawaharlal's life is summed up in this Ghalib verse he quoted in a letter to Indira. A newspaper correspondent described him as a Brahmin, 'a man with a mystical quality of reaching … masses of men, a secret Caesar. He loves the British, he resents Western influence on his life, he is an artist, he is an intellectual snob.' Camping then in Ireland, he told Edwina Mountbatten, 'It is extraordinary how a simple and straightforward person like me should be considered so mysterious.'

Jawaharlal's life had become a long succession of tests, even though he had stolen the limelight very early. He therefore glowed with satisfaction 'at the sight of our nation on the march, realizing its goals one by one'. While watching the Republic Day parade in 1955, he had a sense of fulfillment 'in the air and of confidence in our future destiny'. Two years later, he told the chief ministers:

If we look around to various countries which have recently attained freedom…India compares very favourably with them, both in regard to our stability and the progress we have made in these last ten years. The record is a creditable one, and this is increasingly recognized by other countries of the world'.

Some of these claims were exaggerated. Jawaharlal knew this was so. Speaking at Allahabad, he talked of 'an emptiness and distress at the sorrow that surrounds us'. He knew that only some part of the dreams had come true. He blamed the bureaucracy for being embedded in their old routines, and conceded that his greatest failure as Prime Minister was his inability to change the colonial administration.

Individuals and parties challenged his developmental strategies, especially his undue emphasis on planning, socialism, and heavy industrialization. His own commitment to equal economic justice and opportunities for all was not in doubt, but his government fell far short of what he promised. He talked of the throbbing agony of the masses, but his government's record in reducing poverty was disappointing. The Left parties accused him of making peace with the landlord-bourgeoisie combination, the big business, and the princes. With his natural aversion to the privileged, he could have done away with privy purses and other privileges still enjoyed by the feudal elements, but it was left to Indira Gandhi to complete her father's unfinished agenda.

Wrote Hiren Mukherjee, an otherwise unabashed admirer: 'He was our beautiful but ineffectual angel, beating his luminous wings largely in vain.' Some thought of him as a modern Hamlet, always on the horns of a dilemma that he could not boldly overcome, while others commented on his game of running with the hare and hunting with the hounds. Some party colleagues challenged his political authority, while opposition members assailed both his priorities and the implementation of his policies. Jayaprakash Narayan, who had parted company with the Congress, accused him of building socialism with the help of capitalism, while the Communist Party of India, led by B.T. Ranadive, organized the great Telangana movement and indicted his government for 'compromise, collaboration and national betrayal'. E.M.S. Namboodripad, Jawaharlal's follower until 1931, regarded the Gandhian and Nehruvian legacy as 'by and large negative'. He criticized them for building India on the model of bourgeoisie democracy at the very time when the bourgeoisie system had landed itself into a deep crisis.

Jawaharlal has also been taken to task for being partisan and wobbly in conducting foreign affairs, especially in relation to China. Those who do so argue that the policy of non-alignment lost its credibility following the border war with China in 1962, when India sought military support from the United States. 'In the end,' notes Benjamin Zachariah, one of the many biographers of Jawaharlal, 'the greatest betrayal of Nehru's policies came from Nehru himself, in compromising non-alignment and becoming the "American stooge" of his own rhetoric and his Chinese interlocutors' acid pronouncements.' This judgement is harsh, but there can be little doubt that his policies towards China, so greatly influenced by Krishna Menon, did not stand him in good stead. In August 1963, for the first time in sixteen years in power, his government faced a no-confidence motion in Parliament.

Errors of judgement were unavoidable, but they did not portray Jawaharlal in a poor light. He had the temper and impatience of a very young man when the Oxford-educated Mohammad Mujeeb first heard him at the All Parties Conference at Lucknow in 1928. He found him 'bored and resentful because of the caution of his elders and the irrelevance of what they held to be of importance'. He did not change much thereafter, though he became a little more discreet and cautious in dealing with his adversaries. His strength lay in being committed to pluralism and to the nurturing of a liberal, secular, enlightened polity and society.

His other great asset lay in promoting literature, art, music, science and technology. 'These,' he had once written, 'make our life rich and deep and varied. They teach us how to live.' He privileged science over spirituality, and, what is more, he privileged education over everything else. According to him, the essential and most revolutionary factor in modern life was not a particular ideology but technological advances. This accounts for his taking the lead in setting up laboratories and institutes of technologies. He lived in the present and imagined not so much the past. 'Old as we are,' he once remarked, 'with memory stretching back to the early dawn of human history and endeavour, we have to grow young again in tune with our present time, with the irresistible spirit and joy of youth in the present and its faith in the future.' He wanted people to come to terms with the present with its infinite variety. This was a far cry from the spiritual mumbo-jumbo aired by many of his colleagues.

In late May and early June 1936, Jawaharlal toured Punjab for six days. Both in towns and villages, vast crowds collected to hear him. He received many compliments. Among 'a wilderness of excited compliments the most charming was from a young man who objected to much that was said, but added, *tusi pyare ho te change ho*' (You are dear and good). 'To a whole generation of Indians,' wrote Sarvepalli Gopal, 'he was not so much a leader as a companion who expressed and made clearer a particular view of the present and vision of the future. The combination of intellectual and moral authority was unique in his time.' What made him popular was his ability to persuade the multitude that what they passionately desired was attainable, and that he, through his visualization, was the man to attain it. He acknowledged:

> The world seems a very dark, dismal and dreary place, full of people with wrong urges or no urge at all, living their lives trivially and without any significance … I feel overwhelmed, not so much by the great problems facing us but rather by the affection and comradeship of friends who expect so much from me. A sense of utter humility seized me in the face of this faith and trust.

To M. Chalapathi Rau, the veteran journalist, Jawaharlal was 'not a Lenin or a Jefferson. He was no imitation. He was Jawaharlal and he had no need to be anybody else.' The most abiding recollection of Marie Seton, author of *Panditji: A Portrait of Jawaharlal* (1967), was his expression as he heard an old peasant complain about the officials making life intolerable for the villagers. Jawaharlal bowed his head in shame. 'That he did,' commented Marie Seton, 'explains why India's nameless people relied on him.'

Arnold Toynbee, the historian, met Jawaharlal first in London in the 1930s. Their second meeting took place in New Delhi in the last week of February 1957. He found him to be 'still human and buoyant'. Their third and final encounter was in February 1960, when Toynbee came to Delhi to deliver the second lecture in a series founded in memory of Azad. This time he found Jawaharlal's once buoyant spirit bowed down: 'What time had been unable to do to him had been done to him by China'. The conflict with China had not yet reached a crisis, but that country, in complete disregard of the Prime Minister's friendly overtures, had begun to behave like a bully.

The hero's victory is not his alone; it is a common victory for mankind, Toynbee remarked. He concluded his appraisal with the following remarks: 'Since his death, Jawaharlal Nehru has been suffering the same treatment as T.E. Lawrence. The debunkers have been busy with him. Yet, after the vultures have finished their scavenging work, Nehru, too, will still be the great man that he was— great, though human; human, so lovable.'

The leaves of the book of Jawaharlal's life are closed, but India lives on, as it has done for centuries, and the idea of India—tolerant and inclusive—beckons, as it must do, always and forever. We will see many seasons go by, following each other into oblivion. We will watch many moons wax and wane and the pageant of the stars move along inexorably and majestically. Yet, what Shakespeare wrote of a very different type of man will always apply to Jawaharlal:

> His life was gentle, and the elements
> So mixed in him that Nature might stand up
> And say to all the world, 'This was a man!'

'I grew up a lonely child,' wrote Jawaharlal in *An Autobiography*. He was Motilal's first child, after two sons, to have survived. His sister Sarup Kumari was born when he was eleven years old.

Facing page: Such was Swarup Rani's great passion for her only surviving son that she would go to great lengths to protect him from *nazar* (the evil eye).

Above left: Jawaharlal, aged two, in traditional Kashmiri dress.

Above right: With Motilal (standing facing left) at his thread ceremony (ritual of the Brahman's second birth) in 1902. The duality of his upbringing—a westernized father and deeply religious and superstitious mother—played an extremely important role in the making of Jawaharlal.

Right: The birthplace of Jawaharlal in Mirganj, Allahabad. The Nehrus moved into Anand Bhawan in 1900.

Facing page: With mother Swarup Rani.

Jawaharlal, c. 1892.
Facing page: With a cousin. Loving parents, a happy joint family and the luxuries of an upper class existence ensured that Jawaharlal's childhood was a privileged one. On his birthday, he would be measured against bags of grain which were later distributed amongst the poor.

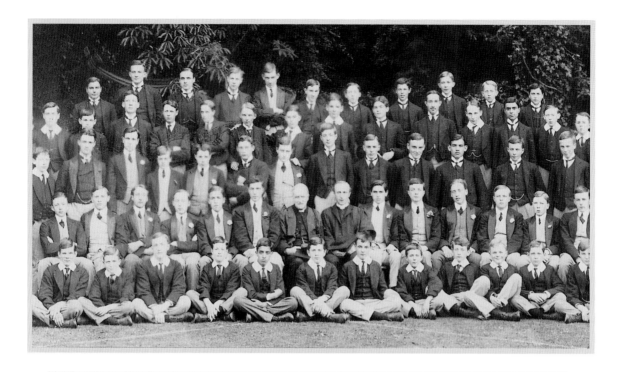

Bath drawers Ties Purse Boots

Harrow School.

It is requested that new boys will bring with them the following clothes at least:

2 black jackets
3 waistcoats
3 pairs of trousers
1 dark overcoat
1 dressing gown
12 day shirts
18 Eton Collars
4 night shirts 2 Pyjamas
3 under vests
3 pairs of drawers
A sponge

9 pairs of socks
18 pocket handk-rchiefs
1 pair of slippers
3 pairs of strong boots
4 sheets
3 pillow cases
6 chamber towels
3 bath towels 6
Tall hat for Sunday use
Brush and Comb
Clothes Brush

On week days a straw hat is worn which may best be obtained in Harrow. Only black neckties are allowed to be worn. It is requested that warm underclothing may be provided during the winter months

Facing page, above: Jawaharlal (second row from top, third from right) was sent to school at Harrow in England when he was sixteen.

Below: The list of clothing students at Harrow were expected to bring.

An excerpt from Jawaharlal's letter to Motilal furnishing details of his personal accounts. In 1911, his expenditure was £800—a large sum at the time.

HARROW SCHOOL.

Payments due in advance from New Boys at the beginning of their First Term.

Name *Nehru*

Account with the Rev. Dr. Wood at the beginning of the *Christmas* Term. *1905.*

	£	s.	d.
Board and Washing	30	0	0
Entrance to House...	10	0	0
Entrance to School	10	0	0
Public Tuition and School Charges	11	16	8
Private Tuition	5	0	0
Bathing Place and Football Field		7	0
Sanatorium and Buildings Fund		10	0
School Music		4	0
Vaughan Library		2	0
Deduct Entrance Scholarship			
TOTAL £	67	19	8

Hearty Greetings
and
Best Wishes for Christmas
and
The Coming Year,
from
J. Nehru.

TRINITY COLLEGE,
CAMBRIDGE.

CHRISTMAS. 1907.

At Harrow, 1906. Motilal would often write to his son and urge him to get himself photographed in the various school uniforms.

Above: Document relating to payment of fee, Harrow, 1905.

Below: Jawaharlal's Christmas card to his parents, sent from Trinity College, Cambridge, in 1907.

Facing page: With Jivan Lal Katju (standing in the last row), Jawaharlal's maternal cousin. Unable to come home for every vacation, Indian boys in England often spent their holidays with English families as lodgers.

Jivan Lal Katju with Jawaharlal seated on his left.

Facing page: Jawaharlal at Trinity College, Cambridge, where he passed with a Second in Natural Science Tripos in 1910.

Facing page: The Nehru family. Krishna Kumari is seated on Swarup Rani's lap, while Sarup Kumari stands next to Jawaharlal. Motilal gave both his daughters a complete upbringing which included riding, dancing and English governesses.

Jawaharlal wrote in his will: 'In the course of a life which has had its share of trial and difficulty, the love and tender care for me of both my sisters, Vijaya Lakshmi Pandit and Krishna Hutheesing, has been of the greatest solace to me.'

TRINITY COLLEGE,
CAMBRIDGE.

Dec 5

I have introduced Mr Nehru to Dr Bond of Trinity College & Trinity Hall. I introduced Mr. Nehru as a man of good character, gentlemanly behaviour. He was likely to be popular & successful. Mr Nehru came here with high commendation from Harrow where he was in the Headmaster's house & in the 5th form. I have a high opinion of Mr Nehru's conduct & diligence.

W M Fletcher
Fellow & Tutor

FORM OF APPLICATION FOR ADMISSION AS A STUDENT
OF THE INNER TEMPLE.

DECLARATION TO BE MADE BY THE APPLICANT.

I, *Jawaharlal Nehru* of *Trinity* College *Cambridge* and of *Anand Bhawan, Allahabad, India* a British subject aged *19*, the *only* Son of *Motilal Nehru* of *Allahabad, India*, in the ~~county of~~ *United Provinces* [Add father's profession, if any, *Advocate High Court* and the condition in life and occupation, if any, of the Applicant.]

Facing page: A letter of recommendation for Jawaharlal's admission to The Inner Temple written by Mr. Fletcher, Tutor and Fellow of Trinity College, Cambridge.

Motilal was keen that his son join the 'heaven born', i.e., ICS. However, seeing Jawaharlal's lack of enthusiasm for the Civil Service, he replaced that hope with him joining the Bar.

Jawaharlal (standing in centre wearing turban) at a fancy dress party in Allahabad. His sisters-in-law, Rameshwari Nehru and Lado Rani Zutshi, can be seen standing fifth and sixth to his right. Motilal's warmth, intellect and generosity attracted people of all communities to his social circle.

MISTRY

Mr. & Mrs. Motilal Nehru request the pleasure of your company on the occasion of the marriage of their son Jawaharlal Nehru with Kamala Kaul, daughter of Pandit Jawaharmal Kaul, at Delhi, on the 7th February, 1916, and afterwards on February 8th and 9th, 1916.

Anand Bhawan, Allahabad

An answer will oblige.

Facing page: Jawaharlal and Kamala (Kaul) were married in grand style at the Haksar Haveli in old Delhi on *Basant Panchami* (which fell on 8 February 1916), a day that heralds the coming of spring. He was 26 and she 17.

Jawaharlal wrote to his father about marriage in 1910: 'You know my likes and dislikes as well as myself and are likely to prove a far better judge (of a bride) ... I do not believe that the aim and object of every man's existence is marriage.'

The Nehru wedding camp in Delhi. As expected, Motilal's only son's wedding was a lavish affair. An exclusive train was hired to take the Nehru clan and friends from Allahabad to Delhi where week-long celebrations took place at a special wedding camp.

Above and facing page: After a long search for a suitable Kashmiri bride for his son, Motilal chose Kamala Kaul, the daughter of a businessman from Delhi. Unlike the Nehru girls, Kamala spoke only Urdu and Hindi. To make the transition smoother and for her to become more compatible with his highly westernized son, Motilal sent Kamala to European governesses to be trained before the wedding. She was taught English and introduced to European manners and habits.

Jawaharlal and Kamala's only child, Indira Priyadarshini, was born twenty-one months after their marriage on 19 November 1917. Indira Gandhi later wrote: 'While my family was not orthodox enough to consider the birth of a girl child a misfortune, it did regard the male child a privilege and a necessity.'

Below: Telegram from Gandhi condoling the loss of Jawaharlal and Kamala's infant son, who died a week after his birth in November 1924.

Facing page: With his niece Nayantara (Vijaya Lakshmi's daughter) on his lap and Indira seated on his right. Indira Gandhi's childhood coincided with Anand Bhawan becoming the centre of a Congress-led national movement.

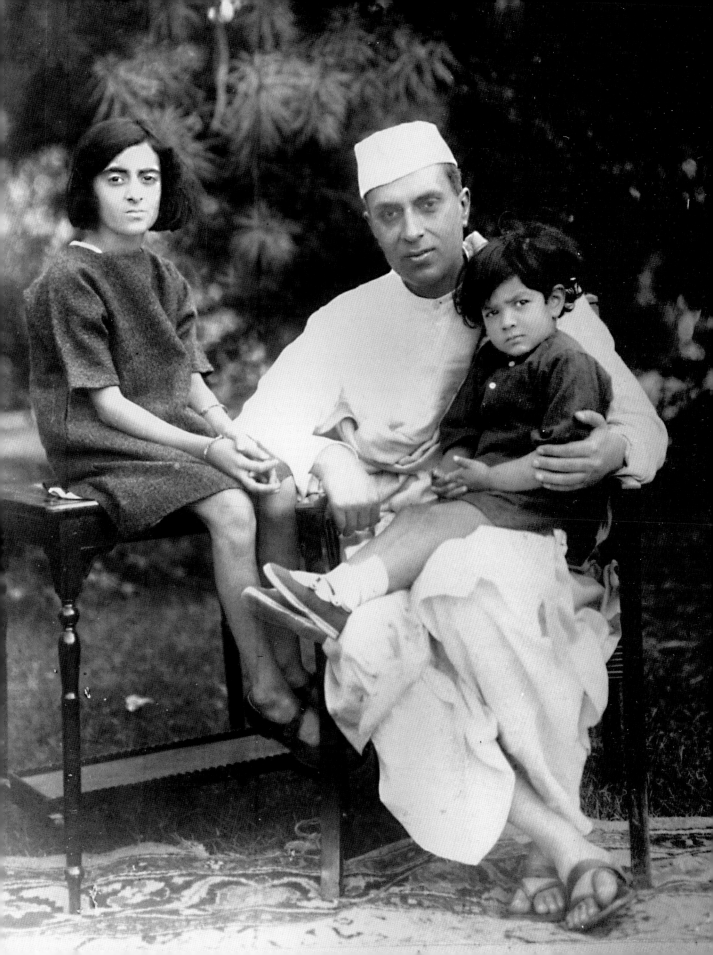

Facing page: With Sarup Kumari. When Motilal decided to join the satyagrahis, women in the Nehru household began to wear homespun clothes, picketed British-run institutions, and spoke at public events.

Krishna Kumari and Sarojini Naidu seated with Jawaharlal to her left, 1929. Sarojini Naidu, the Congress party's second female president and a poetess, remained a close family friend. She became free India's first woman governor.

Jawaharlal's letter to Motilal, 14 August 1920, informing him of his arrest. He begins with the words, 'Greatness is being thrust on me...'

Left: A bullet from Jallianwala Bagh preserved by Jawaharlal.

Jawaharlal behind bars in 1921. He later wrote: 'It seemed to him (father) preposterous that I should go to prison ... Father—I discovered later—actually tried sleeping on the floor to find out what it was like, as he thought that this would be my lot in prison...'

Right: Wooden ticket worn by Jawaharlal as a convict at the District Jail, Lucknow, in 1921.

Facing page: Motilal and Swarup Rani at the wedding of Sarup Kumari (above: from then on she became known as Vijaya Lakshmi Pandit) to Ranjit Sitaram Pandit, a barrister from Rajkot, Gujarat, on 10 May 1921. Their wedding was the last lavish wedding at Anand Bhawan.

Ranjit Pandit was deeply involved in the nationalist movement. When he died on 14 January 1944, Jawaharlal, who was imprisoned at Ahmadnagar Fort at the time, wrote to his sister, 'Ranjit was more than a brother-in-law to me; he was a brother and a comrade.'

In Delhi, 5 March 1931. From left, seated on floor: Sri Narain, Usha, Hanuman Prasad, Bimla, Brij Kishan Chandiwala, Ram Kishan Das and an unidentified person. Seated on chairs: Abdul Qadir Bawazir, M.A Ansari, Vallabhbhai Patel, Syed Mahmud, J.M Sengupta. Middle row: Sri Prakasa, Rajendra Prasad, Mahadev Desai, C. Rajagopalachari, Pattabhi Sitaramayya, Sheo Prasad Gupta, Shankerlal Banker and an unidentified person. Rear row: Shoaib Qureshi, Rajalal, Pyarelal, Ram Gopal, Govind Malaviya, Jamnalal Bajaj, Gopinath Johri, Faridul Haq Ansari, Ratanlal Jain, S.D Upadhyaya, Banwarilal, Motilal and Ramswarup Khanna.

At Birla House, New Delhi, November 1939. 'And then Gandhi came. He was like a powerful current of fresh air that made us stretch ourselves and take deep breaths...' wrote Jawaharlal about Mohandas Karamchand Gandhi who was to become his political and ideological mentor.

Above: Gandhi sends his birthday wishes to Jawaharlal in 1924.

Facing page: Motilal and Jawaharlal at the Lahore Congress, December 1929. Jawaharlal had taken over as president of the Congress from Motilal at this session. In 1928, Motilal wrote: 'If Jawahar lives for ten years he will change the face of India... Such men do not usually live long; they are consumed by the fire within them.'

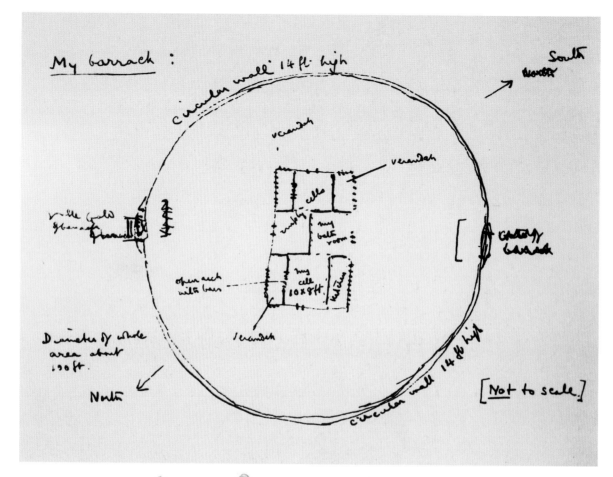

Sketch of Barrack No. 6 from Jawaharlal's prison diary while in Naini Central Prison, Allahabad, in 1930. He was to later write about this particular time in jail: 'Was it my fancy, I wonder, or is it a fact that a circular wall reminds one more of captivity than a rectangular one? The absence of corners and angles add to the sense of oppression.'

Left: Samples of yarn spun in prison in 1941. Jawaharlal wore khadi (which he called the livery of freedom) throughout his life. The family's old tailor, Mohammad Hasan, who had moved from Allahabad to New Delhi, used to mend and darn the Prime Minister's old khadi clothes as Jawaharlal did not like discarding his old clothes.

Facing page: Handwritten corrections to his book *Glimpses of World History*, a compilation of nearly 200 letters to a young Indira about world history.

Glimpses Vol I   47

                    List 'A'   Corrections &c

Page	Line	Present reading	correct reading (as it should read)
[IX	5	Zinda Bad should be one word	Zindabad]
B X	6	ghost	Ghost
XI	No 85	Delete 'The' before 'Sixteenth'	
XII	1	delete 'The' in Governments	
[8,9,10	—	'Zinda bad' throughout these pages – in title – page heading &c – to be one word –]	
B 19	11	'Outer'	Refer to original verify
23	8	Question	Questions
28	16	These	those
34	3,4	The figure for the Hindustanis speaking population given here differs from that given at page 394 line 21. It is desirable to have the same figure – whichever is approximately the more correct.	
42	21	delete , after 'years'	
43	12	'Sun' (second one)	'sun' (small s)
44	22	after 'efries'	comma ,
49	3 from bot	correct	right
53	7	after 'religions'	comma
55	29	The Hindi translator in a note has stated that this tree was not 'peepal' but some other kind. As a matter of fact the tree at Anuradhapura in Ceylon which is supposed to have grown from a branch of the original pipal tree at Gaya, is certainly peepal. This to be verified.	

48

Before the inauguration of the All India Village Industries Exhibition at Tilak Nagar, Faizpur, in December 1936.

Facing page: Jawaharlal with Dr. M. A. Ansari, a prominent physician who had a ward named after him at London's Charing Cross Hospital. He was President of the Congress in 1927. Dr. Ansari was close to the Nehrus and treated both Kamala Nehru and Motilal during their illness.

During the Salt Satyagraha in 1930. From left, standing on the platform: Kamala Nehru, Swarup Rani and Uma Nehru.
With the Nehru women also deeply involved in the nationalist struggle, the family was hardly ever together at Anand Bhawan. Long prison terms and political events in various parts of the country did not make it easy for them to lead a normal family life.

Facing page: Krishna Kumari and Kamala Nehru as volunteers during the civil disobedience movement of 1930. The Nehru women were among the first participants in the movement.

Facing page, top: Motilal's nephews Shridhar and Brijlal (standing first and third from left) with their wives Raj Dulari and Rameshwari (seated first and second from left) in Rangoon. Also seen are Brijlal's sons Braj Kumar (seated in front) and Balwant Kumar (in Rameshwari's lap).
Below, left: Rameshwari and Brijlal.
Below, right: Rameshwari with her sons Braj Kumar and Balwant Kumar (in her lap).

Above, left: Braj Kumar Nehru (Bijju) and his Hungarian bride Fori on their wedding day in 1934. B.K. Nehru became one of India's finest representatives abroad (he was ambassador to America during the Kennedy years and later High Commissioner to the UK) and an outstanding civil servant at home.

Above, right: Brijlal Nehru and Jawaharlal remained close from their days as students in England until the end. Fori Nehru recalls how Jawaharlal (after he himself had suffered a stroke) would visit her father-in-law everyday in hospital. Holding his cousin's hand, he would sit in silence.

Above, left: Uma Nehru (Mrs. Shamlal Nehru) with son Anand Nehru.

Above, right: Shamlal Nehru was named Roman Emperor by family members because of his immaculate dress style and the manner in which he carried a shawl.

Right: Jawaharlal with Uma Nehru, by now an MP, on 2 February 1959, the day Indira Gandhi was elected President of the Congress.

Facing page top, left: Shyam Kumari Nehru (also an MP) with her brother Anand Nehru (Arun Nehru's father) and their dog Bessie, in Simla.

Top, right: Suraj Nehru before her marriage to Anand Nehru. This picture was sent to Motilal to choose a bride for his nephew's son. Suraj Nehru recalls that the first time she met Motilal she fainted because she was so in awe of him.

Below: Shyam Kumari, Indira, Man Mohani Zutshi (Nehru's first cousin Ladli Prasad Zutshi's daughter), Krishna, unidentified.

At the Haripura Congress, 1938. From left: Achyut Patwardhan, Subhas Chandra Bose, Jamnalal Bajaj, Jawaharlal, Acharya Kriplani.

Facing page: In conversation with Gandhi at the Howrah station, Calcutta.

Below: Telegram to Gandhi on 5 May 1933.

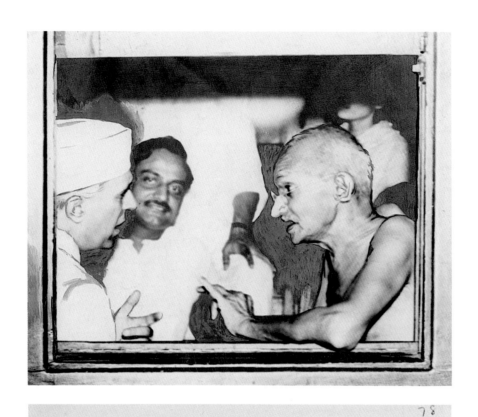

78

Copy of Telegram

Gandhiji
Yeravda Prison Poona

Your letter, what can I say about matters I do not understand
I feel lost in strange country where you are only familiar landmark
and I try to grope my way in dark but I stumble still
whatever happens my love and thoughts will be with you.

Jawahar
5·5·33

Jawaharlal being taken in a specially decorated bullock-cart as Congress President at the Faizpur session of the party. Congress sessions had previously been held in large towns, but in 1936 the village of Faizpur was bestowed the honour of hosting the meeting.

With Sarojini Naidu, Subhas Chandra Bose and B. Satyamurti at the Congress Working Committee meeting at Vithalnagar, 1936.

With Congress leaders, Sardar Vallabhbhai Patel, Subhas Chandra Bose and Acharya Kripalani.

With Sardar Vallabhbhai Patel and Acharya Kriplani at the venue of the Congress Working Committee meeting at Wardha, January 1942.

Singing *Vandemataram* with Gandhi, Maulana Azad, Khan Abdul Gaffar Khan and Sarojini Naidu at the Congress meeting in Wardha, 1942.

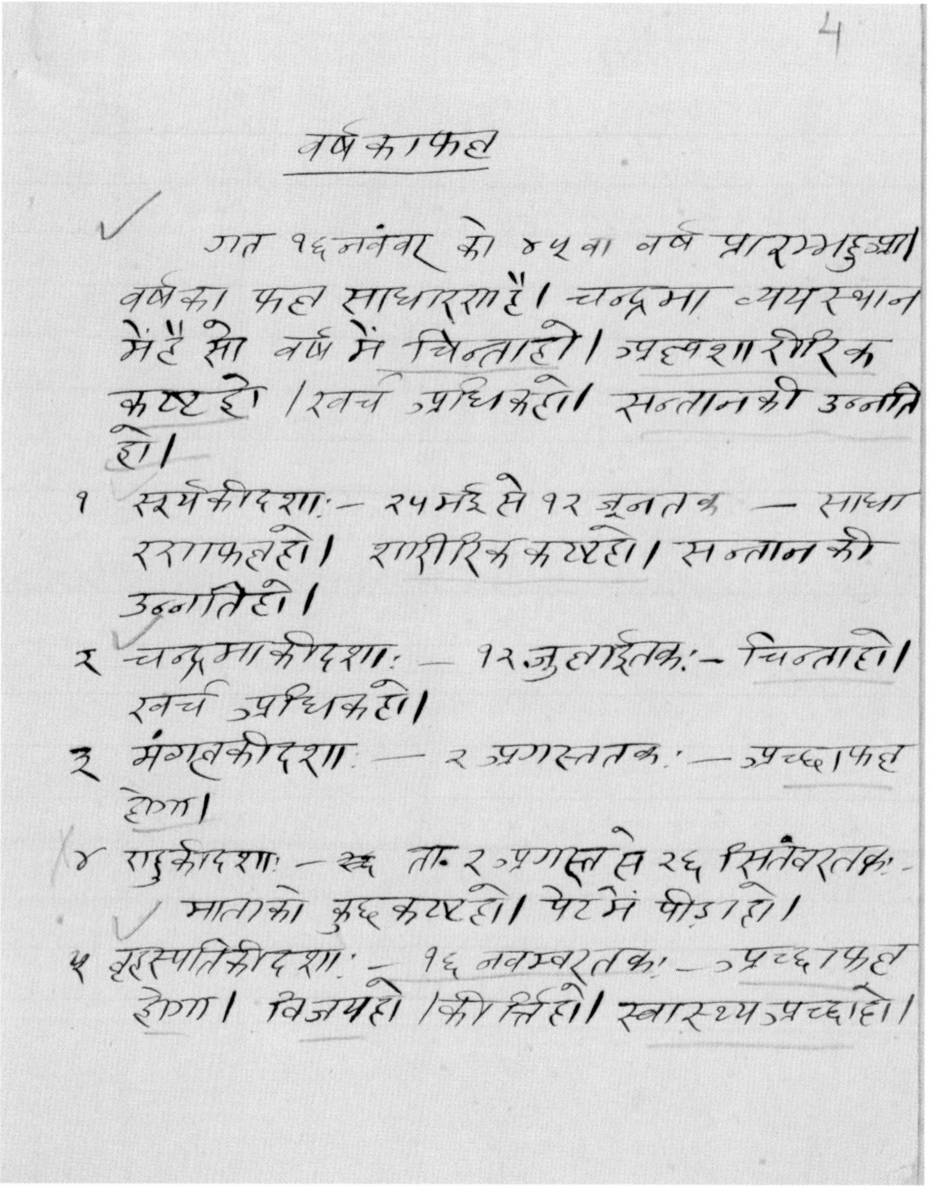

4

वर्ष का फल

गत १६ नवंबर को ४५ वां वर्ष प्रारम्भ हुआ। वर्ष का फल साधारण है। चन्द्रमा व्ययस्थान में है सो वर्ष में चिन्ता हो। अल्प शारीरिक कष्ट हो। खर्च अधिक हो। सन्तान की उन्नति हो।

१ सूर्य की दशा:— २५ मई से १२ जून तक — साधारण फल हो। शारीरिक कष्ट हो। सन्तान की उन्नति हो।

२ चन्द्रमा की दशा:— १२ जुलाई तक:— चिन्ता हो। खर्च अधिक हो।

३ मंगल की दशा:— २ अगस्त तक:— अच्छा फल होगा।

४ राहु की दशा:— ता० २ अगस्त से २६ सितंबर तक:— माता को कुछ कष्ट हो। पेट में पीड़ा हो।

५ बृहस्पति की दशा:— १६ नवम्बर तक:— अच्छा फल होगा। विजय हो। कीर्ति हो। स्वास्थ्य अच्छा हो।

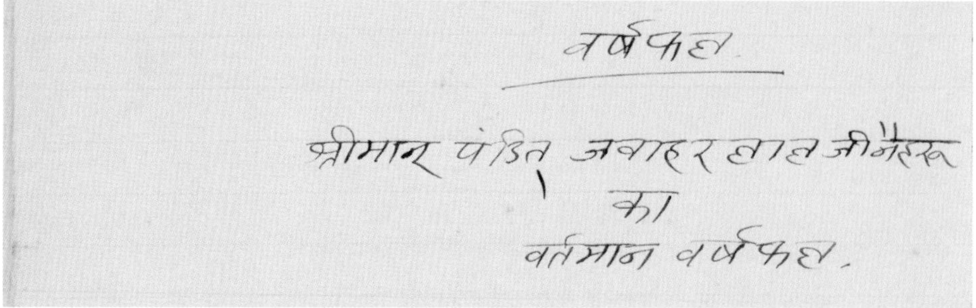

वर्षफल

श्रीमान् पंडित जवाहरलाल जी नेहरू
का
वर्तमान वर्षफल.

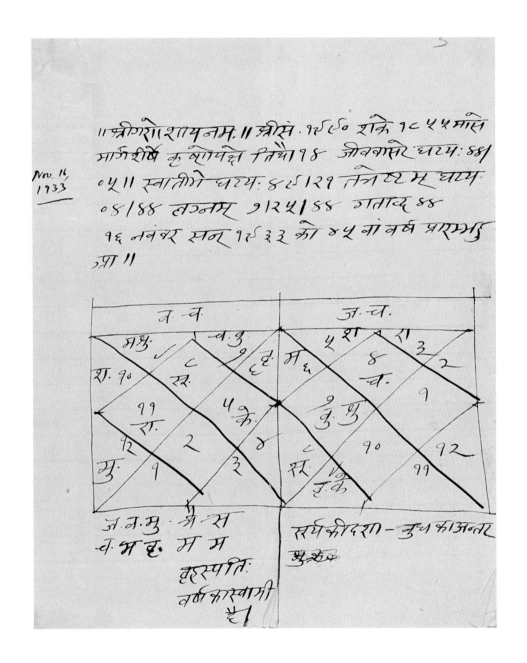

Jawaharlal's horoscope for 1933—apart from mentioning minor ailments which might inflict his mother and wife, the horoscope did not elaborate on his immediate future. It did, however, mention the success of his offspring.

With Bhulabhai Desai and Rajendra Prasad (who became India's first President) during a Congress meeting.

With Acharya Kripalani and Vallabhbhai Patel
at a Congress meeting in Meerut, 21 November
1946.

Despite her failing health, Kamala Nehru participated in politics. Even though she had no access to formal education, she became a strong advocate of women's education. In 1931, when she was arrested, Jawaharlal was delighted and called it a 'wonderful New Year gift'. This picture is dated 1935—less than a year before her death.

Facing page: Kamala Nehru photographed by her husband in 1930. He wrote about his wife after her death in 1936: '...her eager spirit fretted at her inaction and her inability to take her full share in the national struggle. Physically unable to do so, she could neither take to work nor to treatment, and the fire inside her wore down the body'.

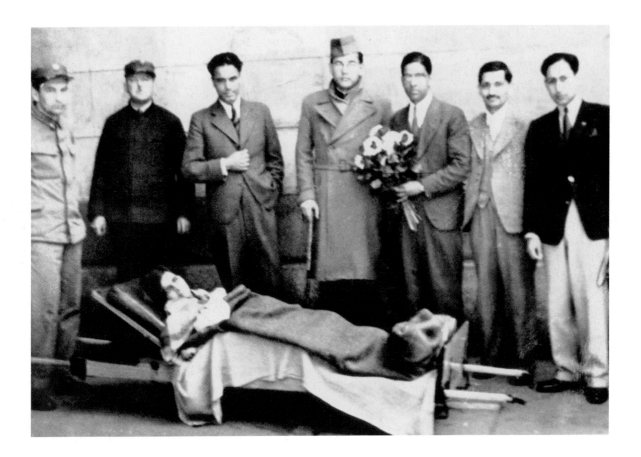

Kamala Nehru at Vienna en route to Berlin for treatment in 1935. At the centre of the group is Subhas Chandra Bose, who visited Indira and Kamala Nehru everyday in Vienna. Indira mentions Bose's kindness during this time, when writing to her father from Europe. Kamala Nehru had been diagnosed with tuberculosis in 1919 and from then on it slowly destroyed her body.

Facing page: Feroze Gandhi and Kamala Nehru met for the first time in 1930. She was then part of a group of women picketing the British-staffed Ewing Christian College in Allahabad. That is where Feroze Gandhi studied. When Kamala Nehru fainted in the midday sun, he came to her aid. Soon after, he signed up as a Congress volunteer and became a regular visitor to Anand Bhawan.

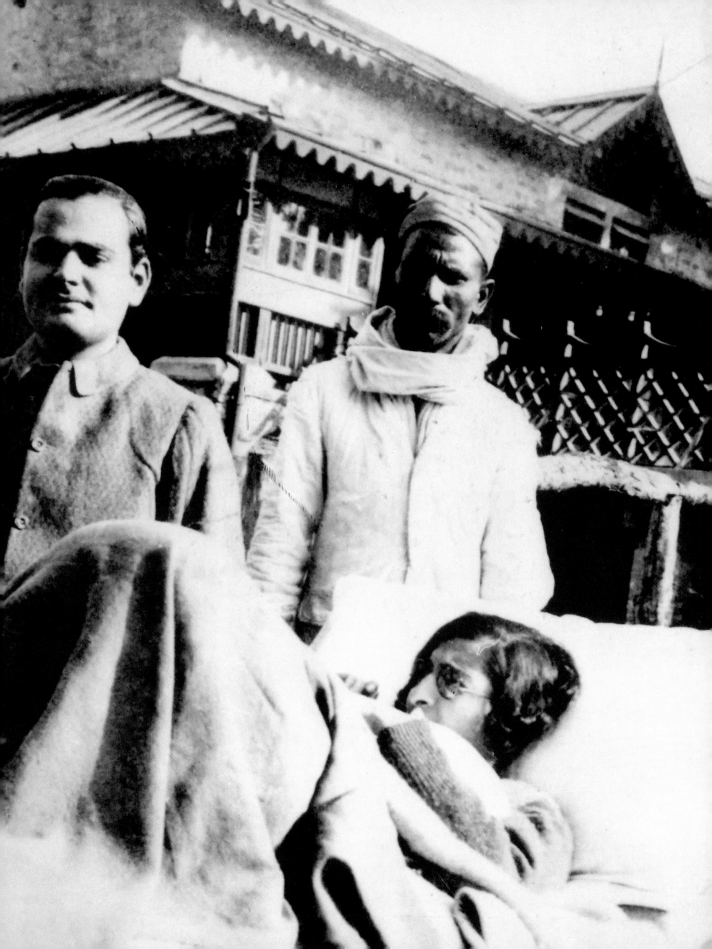

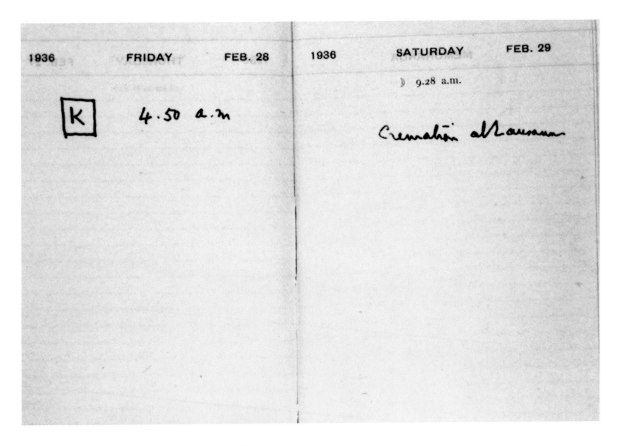

Jawaharlal's diary entry from the time of Kamala Nehru's death. He had recently been made President of the Congress and had planned to return to India from Europe on 28 February 1936—the day Kamala Nehru breathed her last. She was cremated in Lausanne two days later. A bereaved Jawaharlal recalled: 'Kamala and I were unlike each other in some ways, and yet in some other ways very alike; we did not complement each other...Neither of us could like a humdrum domestic life, accepting things as they were...'

Left: Jawaharlal comforting his mother after Kamala Nehru's death.

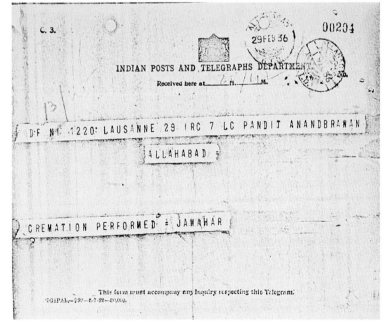

Jawaharlal at Karachi in March 1936 on his return from Lausanne with Kamala Nehru's ashes. Jawaharlal and Kamala Nehru had been married for eighteen years— of which many had been spent apart due to prison terms, illness and their political commitments.

Right: Telegram to waiting family members in Allahabad informing them of Kamala Nehru's cremation.

TO
KAMALA,
WHO IS NO MORE

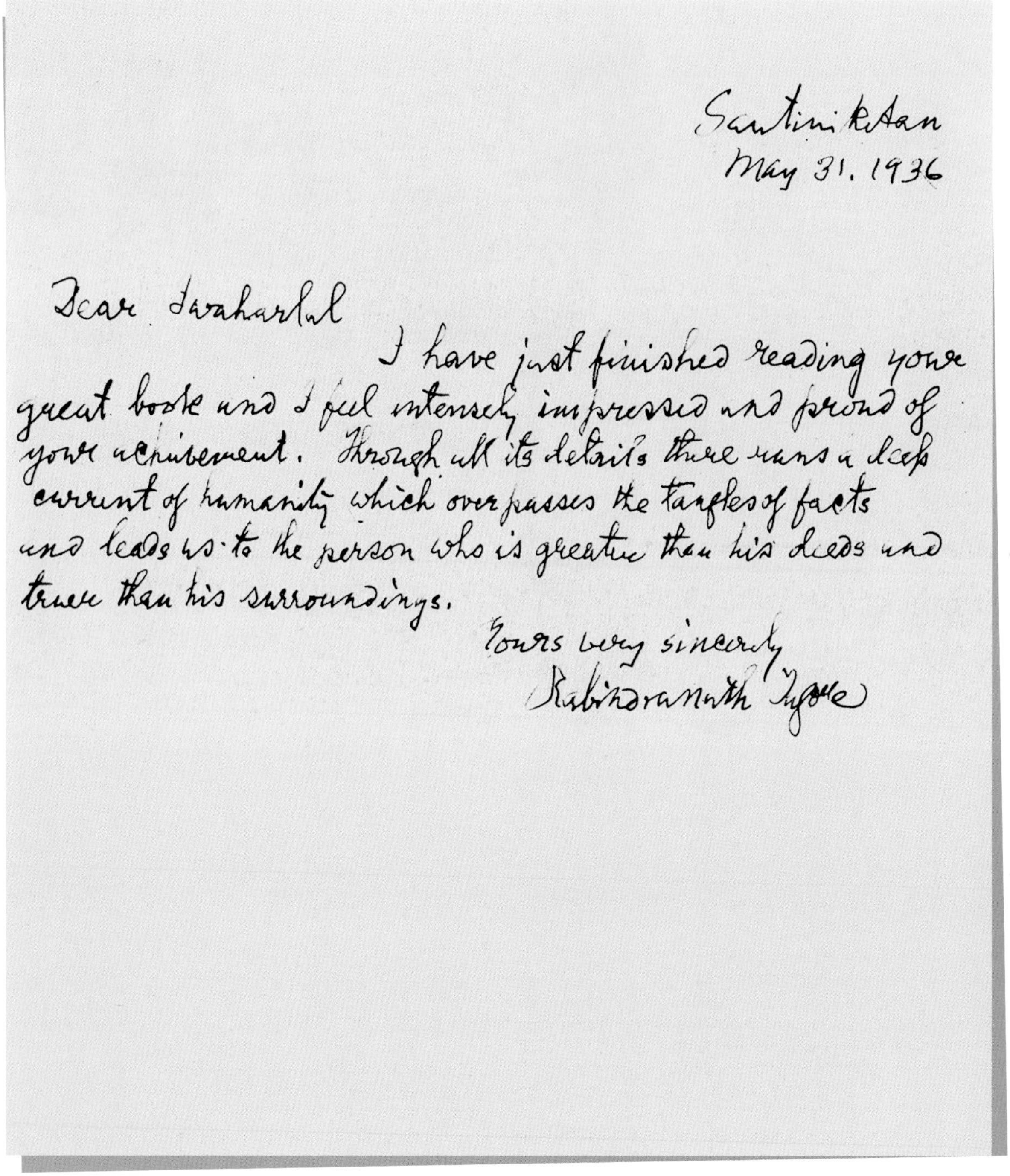

Santiniketan
May 31. 1936

Dear Jawaharlal

I have just finished reading your great book and I feel intensely impressed and proud of your achievement. Through all its details there runs a deep current of humanity which over passes the tangles of facts and leads us to the person who is greater than his deeds and truer than his surroundings.

Yours very sincerely
Rabindranath Tagore

Facing page, top: On cremating Kamala Nehru, Jawaharlal wired his publishers in London. He wanted the dedication for his forthcoming book, *An Autobiography* to read, 'To Kamala, who is no more'.
Below: Tagore's letter congratulating Jawaharlal on his recently published *An Autobiography*.

Jawaharlal had immense regard for Rabindranath Tagore. On 8 March 1936, the poet spoke in memory of Kamala Nehru to the inmates of his ashram in Santiniketan. He referred to Jawaharlal as the *Rituraj*—'representing the season of youth and triumphant joy'.

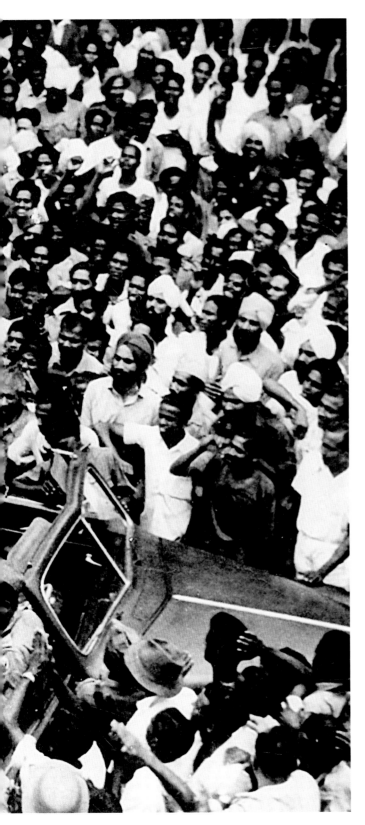

In April 1936, Jawaharlal attended the Lucknow session of the Congress as its President. During the election campaign of 1936–37, he travelled nearly 50,000 miles in 130 days by various modes of transport. His intense efforts resulted in a resounding victory for the Congress in the January and February 1937 elections. The Muslim League only secured 4.4 percent of the Muslim votes—strengthening Jawaharlal's belief that the League's claim of being the sole true representative of India's Muslims was unfounded.

After immersing his mother's ashes in Allahabad on 10 January 1938. Soon after Jawaharlal commented: 'The home that father had built up so lovingly goes to pieces'. Swarup Rani died of a massive stroke in her sleep—her widowed sister Bibi Amma, who had lived with her, died suddenly 24 hours later of a brain haemorrhage.

Facing page: When Swarup Rani suffered blows from a lathi during the National Week of 1932, she wrote to her son who was in Bareilly Jail: 'The mother of a brave son is somewhat like him. It was only a lathi—had it been a gun I would have bared my chest'.

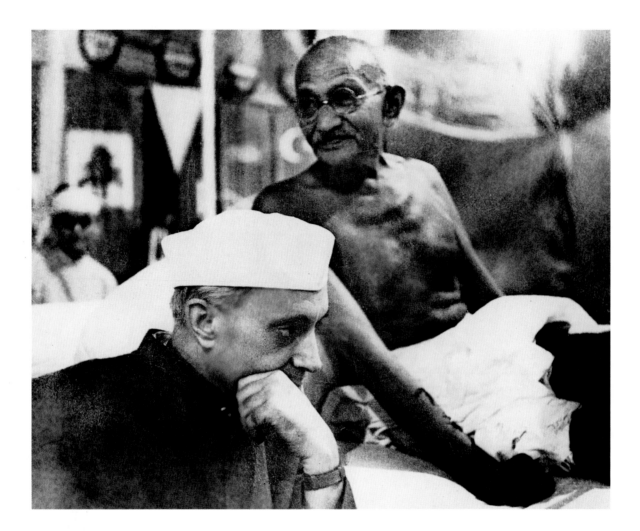

Jawaharlal and Gandhi shared a complex relationship—despite their mutual affection. There were many instances when Jawaharlal was frustrated with Gandhi's unorthodox methods. Yet, he relied on him for support and guidance. Gandhi, in turn, reciprocated with fatherly affection.

Facing page: With Vallabhbhai Patel. While Jawaharlal leaned towards the Left, the latter was seen as a hardliner allying himself with the Right. Despite their differences they made a formidable team. Patel was known as the Iron Man of India because of his determined and forceful leadership as Deputy Prime Minister and Home Minister during the critical first years after Independence.

Facing page: Jawaharlal with Stafford Cripps and Maulana Azad. The British Cabinet Mission visited New Delhi in April 1946. A shared political ideology (anti-imperialism and socialism) turned political acquaintances Jawaharlal and Cripps into lifelong friends.

Liaquat Ali Khan, Jinnah, Baldev Singh, Lord Pethick-Lawrence (Secretary of State for India), Jawaharlal and Krishna Menon at Heathrow Airport, December 1946. The leaders were in England to hold talks with the British Government.

A historic moment in the birth of a new India. On 8 February 1947, Jawaharlal moved the resolution for an independent sovereign republic at the Constituent Assembly in New Delhi.

Mountbatten discusses the plan for the transfer of power at Viceroy's House, New Delhi, 2 June 1947. From left: Communications Member Sardar Abdur Rab Nishtar, Defence Member Sardar Baldev Singh, Congress President Acharya Kripalani, Home and Information and Broadcasting Member Vallabhbhai Patel, Advisor to the Viceroy Sir Eric Melville, Vice President of the Interim Government Jawaharlal, Lord Mountbatten, M.A. Jinnah, (hidden behind Mountbatten) and Finance Minister Liaquat Ali Khan.

Left: At the All India Congress Committee meeting, New Delhi, 15 June 1947. Voting for the partition of India. Seated behind Jawaharlal is G.B Pant.

Facing page: With Jinnah in Simla, 1946. Lord Mountbatten, the last viceroy of India, recalled: 'I asked him (Jawaharlal) about Mr. Jinnah. He gave me a remarkable word-picture of Jinnah's character. He described him as one of the most extraordinary men in history.'

Above: Swimming at the Viceroy's House.

Left: With Edwina Mountbatten. Their friendship continued even after the Mountbattens had retuned to England.

Right: Jawaharlal practised yoga on a regular basis. He wrote in his *Autobiography*. 'Among my exercises one pleased me particularly—the *shirshasana*... The slightly comic position increased my good humour and made me a little more tolerant of life's vagaries.'

Facing page, top: With the Mountbattens as they leave the Viceroy's House for the last time in August 1947.

Below: With the Mountbattens at an official reception at India House, London, 1955.

The first Prime Minister of free India hoists the Tricolour at the Red Fort, Delhi, on Independence Day, 1947.

On 15 August 1947, Rajpath and surrounding official buildings—once the centre of British Imperial power in India—were swarming with crowds of people celebrating freedom from colonial rule.

With Gandhi's body, New Delhi, 30 January 1948. To his right is Muhammad Yunus. Nathuram Godse, a Hindu extremist and member of the RSS, shot the father of the nation three times at a prayer meeting in Delhi.

Facing page: In January 1931 Gandhi had said, '...when I am gone he (Jawaharlal) will speak my language'.

In June 1949 Vijaya Lakshmi Pandit's Wellesley-educated daughter Chandralekha (Lekha) married Ashok Mehta, a young Foreign Service officer. The wedding took place at Teen Murti House—Jawaharlal's official residence in New Delhi. Earlier in the year Vijaya Lakshmi's second daughter Nayantara (Tara) married Gautam Sahgal. The wedding took place in Anand Bhawan.

Facing page: Vijaya Lakshmi had an illustrious political career. She became the first Indian woman to hold a cabinet post in 1937; the world's first woman ambassador when she was appointed ambassador to the Soviet Union in 1947; and was elected the first woman president of the U.N General Assembly for 1953-54 session. She was also ambassador to the United States in 1949 and Great Britain in 1954.

Signing the Constitution of India in New Delhi on 24 January 1950. The day fixed for the proclamation of the Republic was 26 January—a significant date in the political history of India as it also marked the anniversary of the national celebration which Gandhi organized after the Purna Swaraj resolution exactly two decades earlier. The Congress celebrated 26 January as "Independence Day" each year.

With Yugoslavian leader Marshal Josip Broz Tito and Madame Tito at a state banquet given in New Delhi in December 1954. During this visit the two leaders outlined the policy of non-alignment which they, along with Nasser of Egypt, propagated.

Right: India rolled out the red carpet for President Tito of Yugoslavia when he arrived in Bombay in 1964 on a state visit. Here is part of the show staged by the Navy to greet the first head of a foreign state to visit India since Independence. Tito can be seen emerging from between the ranks of the Guard of Honor in foreground while Indian Air Force planes fly low overhead.

One of Jawaharlal's most endearing qualities was his sense of humour and the ability to not take himself too seriously all the time. On his urging his birthday dinner would become a fancy dress party and if a guest came without a costume—the host would lend them something from his collection of national dresses gifted to him during his travels.

With his pet tiger cubs at Teen Murti House, New Delhi. The Nehru family loved animals. While Motilal had kept many dogs and maintained an entire stable of fine Arabian horses in Anand Bhawan, Jawaharlal had dogs, a Red Himalayan panda named Bhimsa and three tiger cubs. In addition, Rajiv Gandhi and Sanjay Gandhi also kept ducks, parrots, turtles and fish at what became a small zoo in the back lawns of Teen Murti House. During his incarceration at Ahmadnagar Fort Prison from 1942–45, Jawaharlal had kept a cat called Chand Bibi.

Right: During his visit to Tokyo in 1957, Jawaharlal called on an old friend, an Indian elephant named after his daughter, which he had gifted to the Japanese children in 1949.

President John F. Kennedy greets Jawaharlal during the latter's visit to America in October 1961. Vice-President Lyndon B. Johnson stands in the background.

Below: Fixing Jacqueline Kennedy's hair, New Delhi, 1962. The Nehru-Gandhi family and the Kennedys have often been compared to each other: the two clans have had their equal share of charismatic leaders, successes and tragedies.

With Albert Einstein in Princeton, New Jersey. Vijaya Lakshmi Pandit, who was the Indian ambassador in Washington at the time, had planned the itinerary for Jawaharlal's visit to America in 1949. This included a meeting with the famous scientist.

Below: In 1955 Winston Churchill wrote to Jawaharlal: 'One of the most agreeable memories of my last years in office is our association...Yours is indeed a heavy burden and responsibility, shaping the destiny of your many millions of countrymen'.

During a Congress session, Jawaharlal displays the playful personality that he was famous for.

Facing page: With G.B. Pant, who served as Chief Minister of Uttar Pradesh and Home Minister of India.

Passport from 1924 described Jawaharlal's profession as 'barrister at law & public affairs'.

Left: Jawaharlal, Vijaya Lakshmi Pandit (then the Indian Ambassador to the U.S) and Indira Gandhi visit the Niagara Falls aboard the famous tourist attraction 'Maid of the Mist' in 1949. They are wearing oilskins to protect themselves from the spray of water.

Facing page, top: Being driven in an old fashioned electric vehicle by Walt Disney during his visit to Disneyland in November 1961.

Facing page, below: During his visit to Denmark in 1957. Jawaharlal and Denmark's premier H.C Hansen partake in boyish adventure.

Jawaharlal driving a tractor during his visit to the Indian Agricultural Research Institute in New Delhi, October 1952.

A barber's bill from Jawaharlal's days at Harrow.

Left: Harrow revisited. On May 2 1960, Jawaharlal returned to his alma mater for a brief visit. Boys cheered him and the masters of the school honoured him.

Facing page: With Khan Abdul Ghaffar Khan (holding Rajiv Gandhi) and Indira Gandhi in Kashmir, 1945. Khan (also known as Frontier Gandhi) was a Pathan from the North West Frontier Province and the leader of Khudai Khidmatgars (Servants of God). After Partition, he moved to Pakistan where his call for a separate Pathan homeland was squelched by the Pakistanis. He died at the age of 98 in 1988 in Peshawar. A year earlier, he received India's highest civilian award, the Bharat Ratna.

With Khan Abdul Ghaffar Khan in Kashmir, June 1940. The two friends set out to climb the highest peak in Kashmir (14,000 above sea level). They reached 12,000 feet where they had their picnic. On his return from this holiday, Jawaharlal wrote in an article, 'Like some supremely beautiful woman, whose beauty is almost impersonal and above human desire, such was Kashmir in all its feminine beauty of river and valley and lake and graceful trees'.

Left: Despite his busy schedule Jawaharlal pursued a wide array of hobbies which included writing, skiing and photography—an interest he shared with his son-in-law Feroze Gandhi and grandson Rajiv Gandhi. He would often escape to Kashmir for short breaks and on several occasions water ski at the Dal Lake in Srinagar.

Below: Taking a picture after a Congress meeting, Lahore, 1940.

Living together at Teen Murti House allowed Jawaharlal to play a formative role in his grandsons's lives. He encouraged them to develop different interests. Rajiv Gandhi attributed his interest in flying to a visit to the gliding club with his grandfather.

Facing page: Jawaharlal and Rajiv Gandhi at Teen Murti House. Against the backdrop of nation building and serious politics there was time for fun also—Rajiv Gandhi and Sanjay Gandhi would often be seen playing with their grandfather in the vast gardens surrounding the Prime Minister's house.

The Tatas and the Nehrus had a long-standing relationship—in January 1928, when Motilal began construction on the new Anand Bhawan, the Tatas sent a specialist engineer to Allahabad to help out. A shared interest in aviation brought J.R.D. Tata and Jawaharlal together. In 1937, with the help of the young J.R.D., Jawaharlal achieved another first—election campaigning by air.

Right: Jawaharlal's love for flying began at Harrow. In 1909 he went to Paris to see the first plane fly over the city and then again in 1927 with Indira to see Charles Lindbergh crossing the Atlantic to land his plane in Paris.

Jawaharlal being cheered by crowds in Beijing
during his state visit to China in 1954.

With Chou En Lai celebrating New Year's eve on a special train which took them from Punjab to Delhi during the Chinese premier's goodwill tour to India in 1957. The Sino-Indo War of 1962 resulted in strong criticism of the Prime Minister's policy of excessive trust in China. Krishna Menon later wrote, 'It had a very bad effect on him. It demoralized him very much.'

Addressing a meeting in Madurai, December 1963. The mild stroke that Jawaharlal had suffered six months earlier seems to tell on his health. Though he continued performing his official duties, he survived only for another six more months, until May 1964.

Left: Leading the Republic Day procession in New Delhi, 26 January 1963.

With Indira Gandhi at Teen Murti House, May 1962.

Right: With Indira Gandhi at Sahasradhara, near Dehra Dun, 25 May 1964. This is the last photograph of Jawaharlal with his daughter. The Prime Minister passed away at 1:44 pm on 27 May 1964 at Teen Murti House. He was 74 years old.

Jawaharlal's funeral cortege goes past the Parliament building on 28 May 1964. The millions who lined the streets of Delhi to bid their leader farewell bore testimony to their tremendous affection for him. In his will he wrote: 'Many have been admired, some have been revered, but the affection of all classes of the Indian people has come to me in such abundant measure that I have been overwhelmed by it'.

Rajiv Gandhi and Sanjay Gandhi before submerging their grandfather's ashes in Allahabad. Rajiv Gandhi was in England and could not make it in time for the funeral. Sanjay Gandhi, then seventeen-years-old, performed the funeral rites.

Facing page: In his will, Jawaharlal asked for most of his ashes to be strewn over every state in India. Indira Gandhi carried out his wish personally and went to Srinagar to scatter her father's ashes over their motherland. A handful was thrown in the Ganga in Allahabad.

When I die I should like my body to be cremated. If I die in a foreign country, my body should be cremated there and my ashes sent to Allahabad. A small handful of these ashes should be thrown into the Ganga and the major portion of them should be disposed of in the manner indicated below. No part of these ashes should be retained or preserved.

My desire to have a handful of my ashes thrown into the Ganga at Allahabad has no religious significance, so far as I am concerned. I have no religious sentiment in the matter. I have been attached to the Ganga and Jumna rivers in Allahabad ever since my childhood, and as I have grown older, this attachment has also grown. She has

been a symbol of India's age-long culture and civilization, ever-changing, ever-flowing, and yet ever the same Ganga. She reminds me of the snowy peaks and the deep valleys of the Himalayas, which I have loved so much, and of the rich and vast plains below, where my life and work have been cast.

Jawaharlal's handwritten will.

The Ganga has

been to me a symbol and a memory of the past of India, running into the present, and flowing on to the great ocean of the future. And though I have discarded much of past tradition and custom, and am anxious that India should rid herself of all shackles that bind and constrain her, and divide her people, and suppress vast numbers of them, and prevent the free development of the body and the spirit; though I seek all this, yet I do not wish to cut myself off from that past completely. I am proud of that great inheritance that has been, and is, ours, and am conscious that I too, like all of us, am a link in that unbroken chain, which goes back to the dawn of history in the immemorial past of India. That chain I would not break, for I treasure it and seek inspiration from it. And in witness of this desire of mine, and as my last homage to India's cultural inheritance, I am making this request that a handful of my ashes be thrown into the Ganga at Allahabad to be carried to the great ocean that washes India's shore.

THE NEHRUVIAN LEGACY
triumphs and tragedies

In July 1966, some months before the general elections, Marie Seton, Jawaharlal's biographer, observed: 'Equally candid, yet equally reticent as she is, it is still too early to judge, or even predict, if she [Indira Gandhi] can evolve a decisive policy and be able to inspire its implementation through the strength of her personal relationships.' Seton would have expressed much less scepticism had she visited India a decade later when Indira Gandhi's leadership skills astounded party colleagues and analysts. The best in her came out in dealing with political and personal adversities.

Did her power of endurance come from Kamala Nehru, who in times of crisis rose above herself and her physical limitations? Opinions differ. Yet, there is no doubt that, in a life so full of tragedies and triumphs, Indira Gandhi, like her father, bequeathed a mixed but vibrant legacy to her party and the nation.

Drawing a fair balance sheet of her achievements and shortcomings is not possible. At the same time, there is no denying that she consolidated what she inherited from her father, raised the country's profile in the comity of nations, and infused dynamism into the Congress party in her early days before it became a tool in the hands of a coterie. She began her term energetically, selflessly and was motivated by the mission to serve the nation. Soon enough, she noticed the ideological inertia in her own government, the bureaucracy's stranglehold, and the factionalism in her party. The same problems had afflicted her father's government.

Born in 1917, Indira was Jawaharlal and Kamala's only child. She was shy, reticent and glum

Facing page: In the spring of 1966, soon after her election as India's Prime Minister, Indira Gandhi, along with her sons Rajiv Gandhi and Sanjay Gandhi, visited Paris.

in her youth. Her concerned father, who had dreamt of her 'putting brick in the building of the India of our dreams', urged her, from the Bareilly District Jail in March 1932, to get rid of 'melancholy and its brood'. In 1931, he had admitted her to the Pupil's Own School in Poona, and thereafter, to Santiniketan, a place where Rabindranath's 'spirit seemed to roam and hover over one and follow one with a loving though deep watchfulness'. Here, too, the young Indira would lapse into her usual feeling of isolation and loneliness. 'It is awful,' she wrote on 16 September 1934, 'when surrounded by crowds and amidst all their chattering and playing, their rowdiness and noise, one has the feeling of being alone.'

Indira, who had nursed her mother at a sanatorium in Bhowali in the Himalayas and later at Badenweiler in Germany, told 'Darlingest Papu' on 21 November 1936: 'I have been trying to analyze my loneliness. It is I think due to my not having any real friend.' At Somerville College, Oxford (1937-1939), she came into contact with radical and left - wing Indian students, some of whom were connected with the Indian Majlis and the University Labour Club. Krishna Menon drew her into socialist and anti-imperialist work in London. She learnt much, acquired new skills, and, above all, gained in confidence. By this time, she had a close friend in Feroze Gandhi, who was educated in Allahabad where his father Jahangir Gandhi had set up a liquor and provision business. They were married on 26 March 1942, despite the strong opposition to their intercommunity marriage.

Through much of her teens, 'exceptional people' had surrounded Indira. That helped her draw inspiration from them and form ideas about the world around her. Reading the Joan of Arc by night, she lectured the household servants by day and, in between, found the 'Monkey Army' to carry messages in and out of jail. In 1929, she travelled with her father, the president-elect, to the Congress session in Lahore. She read the Purna Swaraj resolution, only to be told by her father, 'Well now that you have read it, you too are committed to it.' During civil disobedience, she felt part of the political excitement that gripped the Nehru women. When Gandhi fasted against the Poona Pact on 20 September 1932, she too fasted and held prayers. A decade later, when she tasted life in prison during the Quit India Movement, she confided: 'My inside is steadily getting tougher. And I think I can honestly thank whatever gods may be for my unconquerable soul.' In another letter on 19 April 1943, she described a 'lovely dream… walking on a deep path':

> I had a feeling that it was suspended in the air although there was nothing to show it positively. And in a perfect circle all around-far away as if there was no obstacle to prevent me seeing the whole horizon at the same time—there was a chain of mountains. All sorts of mountains: high towering into the sky besides smaller ones, ragged and smooth, snow-covered and bare. And on a single peak in front of me there was a dazzlingly beautiful light. It seemed like a spotlight from above although the sky was pitch dark, neither sun, nor moon nor stars. It was awe-inspiring. I was looking at it and walking on and on when the road became narrow and covered with deep snow like a mountain pass. I woke up feeling exhilarated and fresh, as if I had been to the Mont Blanc or the Matterhorn at least.

Feroze, also jailed, was set free on 8 July 1943. He and Indira spent a few days at a hill station near Bombay before returning to Anand Bhawan. Jawaharlal thought well of him, entrusted him with family and political responsibilities, and commended the dynamism he introduced in running the Congress newspaper, *The National Herald*. After Independence, he was elected to free India's first Lok Sabha by the voters of Pratapgarh and Rae Bareilly. But his premature death on 8 September 1957 abruptly ended his parliamentary career.

While Feroze pursued his parliamentary duties, for which he received deserved acclaim, Indira Gandhi, a lady of great charm, filled in as hostess in place of her mother and ran the wheels of her father's house smoothly. Political and social work, too, interested her. Hence, she chaired the Central Social Welfare Board (1953-57), served the Working Committee and Central Election Committee (1955), Central Parliamentary Board (1956), and presided over the All India Youth Congress (1956 to 1960). She found the experience of being the Congress President 'exhilarating at times, depressing at times, but certainly worthwhile'. In general, she was 'not terribly concerned with public acclamation or the reverse'. Chairing a Congress session or delivering an address had no special meaning or attraction for her.

Long years before, on 30 May 1933, Jawaharlal had written to her that it was not right to shut one's eyes to difficulties and problems, and that it would not do to follow the example of the ostrich and bury one's head in the sand. When Lal Bahadur Shastri died in January 1966, soon after signing the Tashkent Agreement with the President of Pakistan, the Congress party's patriarchs—derisively called the 'Syndicate'—chose her as their leader. She agreed to wear the crown of thorns, and showed, contrary to many people's expectations, no sign of nervousness in holding the high office. She was supremely confident, endowed with special gifts that soon came to light. Presumably, her role model was no other than Jawaharlal, who had warned that running away from trouble was 'unworthy and undignified', and that moping and nursing a grievance secretly betrayed weakness and folly. Without expending her energy on petty matters, she consolidated her political power in no time. It was an extraordinary start to a controversial career.

From the very beginning, powerful forces were at work to erode her position. To the Syndicate, therefore, her first veiled message was to pack their bags or to accept her authority. It took a while before she achieved this. She asserted herself over Morarji Desai, her principal *bête noire*, in the choice of her candidate, Zakir Husain, to the Republic's Presidency. Nationalization of the fourteen commercial banks, abolition of privy purses, a vigorous policy of land reforms, ceiling on personal income, private property and corporate profits, and the *garibi hatao* campaign raised her estimation in the public well beyond anybody's imagination. In 1969, the 'Great Split' between the Congress of Indira Gandhi and the Congress (O) of Nijalingappa had already taken place. It is justly regarded as a milestone in Indira Gandhi's development as well as Indian political history.

1971 began with a landslide Congress victory in the general elections, followed by India's decisive triumph in its war with Pakistan in December 1971. Indira Gandhi signed the Simla Agreement with Zulfiqar Ali Bhutto, the President of Pakistan, in 1972, and placed India firmly, if controversially, on the international map by exploding a nuclear device

at Pokhran two years later. On the Western front, even in times of extreme isolation as in 1971, she dealt with leaders like Richard Nixon, President of the US, on equal terms.

She was the elected empress of India. Millions worshipped her as an incarnation of Shakti or compared her with the all-powerful Hindu goddess, Durga, a comparison made permanent in a series of murals M.F. Husain painted. Meanwhile, a crisis was brewing all around her owing to two bad monsoons, the rise in crude oil prices, and the scarcity of water and oil. The victory of 1971–1972 had made the Congress party complacent, especially in Gujarat and Bihar, and issues of governance were, consequently, relegated to the background.

Public discontent expressed itself in strikes and demonstrations, particularly the famous railway strike of May 1974, and the opposition parties, having been virtually annihilated in the 1971–1972 elections, exploited the opportunity. Jayaprakash Narayan, a charismatic figure who had eschewed active politics for eighteen years and had instead concentrated on the Bhoodan Movement, led them. For once in her public career, the daughter of Jawaharlal was pushed into a corner. Added to her growing woes was the Allahabad High Court judgment on 12 June 1975 that found her guilty of using government officials for political purposes. Compared to the scale of electoral malpractices in the previous parliamentary and state elections, this was a trivial electoral misdemeanour. But the opposition parties, a disparate coalition of leaders who subscribed to conflicting ideologies, found an excuse to demand the Prime Minister's resignation. The demand was unfair, and yet in the build-up to the High Court verdict and in its aftermath, the opposition, especially the Jana Sangh leaders who had an almost pathological dislike for the Nehrus because of their liberal and secular commitments, discarded the established parliamentary norms that applied to a democratically elected leader.

The upper echelons of the Congress leadership was seized with panic and prevailed upon Indira Gandhi to impose a national Emergency on 25 June 1975. Why? She told Mohit Sen, the veteran Communist leader, that the 'total revolution' was meant to destroy Indian democracy by spreading anarchy and chaos. She regretted the hurt caused to innocent people but not the proclamation of the Emergency itself. At the end of this meeting, 'her unadorned beauty, unaffected charm, natural courtesy, sense of ease and her ability to put the other person at ease simply by taking him seriously', impressed Mohit Sen.

Whatever the provocation, to which Indira Gandhi dwelt at length, the Emergency should not have been promulgated, particularly because such a drastic decision had to be backed by constitutional amendments, the imposition of President's rule in Gujarat and Tamil Nadu, the arrest of political leaders, and the imposition of press censorship. It was not necessary to take such extreme steps to deal with a ramshackle coalition of power-hungry politicians led by an ailing Jayaprakash Narayan, who found himself between the devil and the deep sea. Moreover, a handful of zealots invited more trouble for Indira Gandhi when they resorted to forced sterilization on the poor, evicted urban squatters and slum dwellers in Delhi, and persecuted workers by freezing their wages or doing away with their services.

The political uncertainties continued until 18 January 1977 when Indira Gandhi went on air in an unscheduled broadcast and in a calm, matter-of-fact voice, remarkably free of rhetoric, broke the news of an election. Democracy had been put back on the rails. Soon thereafter, the Janata Party came into existence, and its four constituents—the Congress (O), the Bharatiya Lok Dal, the Jana Sangh and the Socialist Party—created a joint command of which the stern, ascetic Morarji Desai was appointed chairman and Charan Singh, the Jat leader from western Uttar Pradesh, its deputy chairman. The combination worked: the Janata Party stormed through the Congress bastions, notching up an astoundingly large number of victories.

The government that came to power appeared to be a divided house. Instead of chartering a radically new course to resolve political and economic problems, the Janata Party acquired a reputation for its intrigues, bickering and power struggle. Jayaprakash Narayan, who had galvanized the non-communist parties to merge into the party and fight what was described as the second battle for freedom, found himself on the sidelines. Soon enough, the writing on the wall was clear. A newspaper report on 6 February 1979 put it thus:

> As mounting labour unrest and caste and religious violence sweeps across India, many people are looking back at former Prime Minister Indira Gandhi's tough Emergency rule with something like nostalgia. Some of the harshest measures of the Emergency have almost been forgotten, or at least do not arouse the same hostility as three years ago.

On 14 January 1980, after a thirty-three-month break, the sixty-two-year-old Indira Gandhi returned to power on the strength of the slogan 'Elect a Government That Works'. 'The Indian Public… has come of age. It demands results and is aware of the power of the ballot,' commented *The Hindustan Times*. Jagjivan Ram, who missed becoming the country's first 'untouchable' leader, hailed her as 'Lok Priya' (the people's favourite) and said her comeback was 'magic or miracle'. All through this period thirty-three-year-old Sanjay Gandhi, who had contested and won election as an MP from Amethi, remained on her side. 'There was concerted effort to make me out to be a cretin unfit for politics,' he said of the previous government's campaign against him. Now, the electorate had provided the man, dressed in hand-spun white cotton pyjamas and loose knee-length kurta, the opportunity of helping his mother realize her dreams for the less privileged Indians.

Indira Gandhi inherited a tottering economy with shortages, spiralling prices and declining industrial and food production. The agitation against the 'foreign immigrants' gathered momentum in Assam, whereas tribal guerillas in Manipur and Mizoram had stepped up their fight for independence. In 1980, students and local political groups boycotted the state assembly and parliamentary elections in Assam amid violent protests. In 1983, a massive upsurge in the state followed a breakdown in the government's negotiations with agitation leaders on their demand to disenfranchise and evict illegally settled immigrants, mainly Muslims, from neighbouring Bangladesh. Widespread violence occurred in early February as militant Assamese plunged their oil-producing state into anarchy.

Militancy in Punjab also acquired ominous proportions from the early 1980. It was fuelled, among others, by Zail Singh, Home Minister, who meddled in Sikh affairs with a view to retaining his strong foothold in Punjab politics. In the process, he backed a Sikh extremist, Sant Jarnail Singh Bhindranwale. In mid-1982, Bhindranwale took refuge in the Golden Temple in Amritsar and unleashed his reign of terror in Punjab. In May 1984, Sikh extremists occupied the Golden Temple in Amritsar and converted it into a haven for terrorists. Indira Gandhi sent the army into the Golden Temple on 5 June 1984. This was Operation Blue Star. Sonia is reported to have said, 'A shadow entered our lives.' On 31 October 1984, Indira Gandhi's own Sikh bodyguards assassinated her. The 'Indira era' was over. President Zail Singh, her own protégé, invited Rajiv Gandhi to form a government. Meanwhile, all hell broke loose as violence against the Sikhs erupted in Delhi, Kanpur in UP, and Bokara in Bihar.

From the day she was sworn in as India's third prime minister on 24 January 1966 to the day of her assassination, Indira Gandhi ruled in her own distinct style and left an indelible mark on Indian politics. To Mohit Sen, her record, at least since 1959, was that of 'a person whose life was politics conceived as service to India and its people as she understood their interests to be'. In the words of Pupul Jayakar, her biographer, she had one major concern at the end of her life: 'whether India could survive with its wisdom intact, for without that wisdom what was India?' She died having posited the question without finding an answer.

Jawaharlal's favourite passage by George Bernard Shaw ran as follows:

> This is the true joy of life, the being used for a purpose recognized by yourself as a mighty one; the being thoroughly worn out before you are thrown on the scrap heap; the being a force of nature, instead of feverish, selfish little clod of ailments and grievances, complaining that the world will not devote itself to making you happy.

'I think I was very conscious of being related to my grandfather,' Rajiv Gandhi told an interviewer in 1989. That he was. But he and brother Sanjay coped with their family inheritance differently.

Born in Bombay on 20 August 1944, 'Rajiv' was chosen as his name because it means 'lotus' in Sanskrit, as does Kamala, the name of Jawaharlal's wife. He went to Doon School at the age of eleven. Five years later, his father died. After staying in Cambridge, where he met his future wife, the Italian-born Sonia Maino, he returned to India. Having trained as a pilot, he joined the Indian Airlines, and married Sonia in Delhi in February 1968. Opting for a quiet life, he showed no interest in politics. But his destiny changed when Sanjay died in a flying accident on 23 June 1980, leaving behind his widow, Maneka, and their infant son, Varun.

Sanjay's tragic death left his mother lonely. Moreover, it made her vulnerable to the sustained attacks and campaigns of her detractors. Many of her friends had deserted her. Aunts and cousins, who had nursed their grievances over personal and family matters, were no longer on her side. That is why the mother prevailed upon her son to share the weighty burden of running the government and keeping the party intact. After a great deal of soul-searching, Rajiv Gandhi agreed to contest elections. Success came easy and he was elected to the Lok Sabha from Amethi on 15 June 1981. In October 1984, he became Prime Minister. The challenges facing him were huge; so were the opportunities.

There can be no doubt that Rajiv Gandhi's remarkable victory at the hustings in 1984—giving the Congress a record majority in the Lok Sabha that even Jawaharlal had not secured—was achieved against the background of the tremendous wave of sympathy in the wake of the brutal gunning down of his mother. At the same time, it must be said that the electorate voted massively for the Congress to express its faith in a leader who, representing the modern face in politics, promised to scale new heights of progress and change. He was young, charming, and, above all, enjoyed the reputation of being 'Mr. Clean' and 'Mr. Decent'.

When circumstances conspired to draw Rajiv Gandhi into the whirlpool of politics, he gave sufficient evidence of his determination to bring in a whiff of fresh air in the political domain. In the early years, especially from 1985 to 1986, his initiatives rekindled great hopes. He struck a chord with the people who approved of, for example, his desire to root out corruption, banish the power brokers, and send the *Aya Rams Gaya Rams* into hibernation. Side by side, he promised to revive the democratic processes in the Congress by holding organizational elections. Here was passionate idealism, and much of Rajiv Gandhi's domestic policy—at least in the early years—was tempered by it.

'Together we will build an India of the twenty-first century,' he pledged to the nation over television and radio. Continuing with the tradition of his grandfather and mother, both of whom established and supported scientific research institutes, he talked of promoting scientific and technological development. More importantly, he wanted such progress to be used to fight poverty. 'The litmus test for any scientific activity in India,' he said, 'is how far it helps to remove poverty.' Thus, he conceived of the most basic technology mission to provide drinking water to every village. With the help of Sam Pitroda, a graduate of Baroda University and the Illinois Institute, he also developed various telecommunication projects.

Rajiv Gandhi's economic liberalization programme spurred the rate of growth. He ran a halfway house between Nehruvian socialism and the promise of a high-tech twentieth-century India. He nudged India out of its moribund systems; indeed, the moves towards liberalization changed the terms of economic debates.

In much of what he said, Rajiv showed a fair degree of commitment to the poor. Thus the sixth Five Year Plan envisaged the reduction of the percentage of people below the poverty line to less than 10 per cent by 1994–5. During his years of office, anti-poverty programmes continued, while the Jawahar Rozgar Yojna was a new rural employment scheme that had to be implemented through village panchayats. In addition, his major initiative for the rural areas was the 64th Amendment to the Constitution, providing for the devolution of power to the panchayats. Finally, the seventh Five Year Plan (1985–90) drew the voluntary sector into the development process and allocated additional funds for NGO work.

The Prime Minister sought to restore the consensual approach to national problems and opted for negotiations to tackle the seemingly intractable issues in Punjab and the Northeast. These resulted in the Punjab, Assam, and Mizo accords—all in his first year in office in 1985. Although some of these accords did not go very far, the initiatives in themselves demonstrated the Prime Minister's inclination to promote dialogue rather than confrontation. On Kashmir, though the crisis remained unresolved, he at least initiated the process for bridging the gulf between the Congress and the ruling National Conference.

In the realm of foreign policy, Rajiv Gandhi pursued his mother's initiative of mobilizing the six nations in search of nuclear disarmament. Thereafter, he launched a crusade against the 'Star Wars' programme. He also signed the historic Delhi Declaration with Mikhail Gorbachev in 1986 that lent a powerful impetus to the nuclear disarmament talks between the US and the Soviet Union. The action plan he placed before the UN in 1989 had a similar impact. These efforts were capped by three other major initiatives: first, giving a new direction to the non-aligned movement in the changing global environment by reinforcing its unity; second, mending fences with Pakistan through talks with Benazir Bhutto in 1988; and third, improving ties with China. His visit to Beijing in 1988 raised hopes of a breakthrough in the border negotiations.

These were impressive achievements. Suddenly, though, a storm over an arms deal, the Bofors issue, broke out in March 1987. The crisis deepened until the electorate passed its verdict against the Congress in 1989. The Rajiv Gandhi dream slowly soured, and, owing to the stridency of the opposition parties, his nation-building projects were relegated to the background. His own ministerial colleagues some of whom were identified with corruption, sycophancy and casteist politics, wronged him. They did not carry out many of the promises, including internal reforms in the Congress party. Rajiv Gandhi conceded: 'I should have stuck to my guns and gone through with them, but it got very complicated and we backed down.' Overenthusiastic bureaucrats in his office distanced him from the people. Soon enough, Punjab, Kashmir and Assam, once spectacular symbols of success, turned into forlorn signposts to failure.

The drought of 1987 was accompanied by a fiscal crisis. That very year India was drawn into the Sri Lankan imbroglio. Although the government managed to overcome the drought, the Sri Lankan venture became a quagmire. No one could satisfactorily explain India's presence in Sri Lanka, even though some point to the Indian Army's success in marginalizing the Liberation Tigers of Tamil Ealam (LTTE) and the conduct of Provincial Council elections as major gains.

In December 1985, Rajiv Gandhi had sounded the tocsin against the power brokers in the party during the Congress centenary celebrations. After describing himself as a mere 'apprentice in the great school of politics', he complained of 'the brokers of power and influence, who ride on the backs of millions of ordinary Congress workers, dispensing patronage to convert a mass movement into a feudal oligarchy'. These cliques, he added, had reduced the Congress to a shell from which the spirit of service and sacrifice had been emptied. He talked of corruption as 'the hallmark of leadership', and of the 'flagrant contradiction between what we say and what we do'. But, as the Bofors crisis and the internal party crisis acquired volcanic proportions,

he began to rely more and more on the power brokers, who had scant respect for popular leaders or the programmes for the poor.

The sudden onset of elections—nineteen months after Rajiv was thrown out of power— recharged his old batteries. He was the only vote-catcher in a crowd of sycophants and self-seekers, the sole Congress politician *en rapport* with the voters. He conveyed the image of being sincere and earnest. Sadly, however, he could not nurture his vision of India. While campaigning in Tamil Nadu, a suicide bomber took his life on 21 May 1991. The tragedy is that he died just when he had the chance to make up for that first term. And perhaps, he would have.

Today, Rajiv Gandhi is remembered for taking India into the twenty-first century (though he talked of preparing for the twentieth). He was a modernizer with strong liberal and secular instincts, though he erred in pushing through legislation on the issue of maintenance for divorced Muslim women. He showed great concern for the poor and responded positively to proposals for alleviating poverty. But his will crumbled with adversity, and his popularity waned owing to the relentless campaigns against him.

In the mid-1950s, Donald Eugene Smith, the political scientist, concluded his important study on the secular state with the observation:

> It is meaningful to speak of India as a secular state. ... India is a secular state in the same sense in which one can say that India is a democracy. ... Despite various undemocratic features of Indian politics and government,

parliamentary democracy is functioning, and with considerable vigour. Similarly, the secular state; the ideal is clearly embodied in the Constitution, and it is being implemented in substantial measure. The question must be answered in terms of a dynamic state which has inherited some difficult problems and is struggling hard to overcome them along generally sound lines.

Secular democracy, in contrast to the Islamic theocracy in neighbouring Pakistan, was in place by the time Jawaharlal died in 1964. Built on substantial historical foundations, India's democratic fabric did not rest on V.D. Savarkar, the father of the language of *pratishodh* and *pratikaar*, all synonyms for revenge, retribution and retaliation, or on Guru Golwalkar's *Bunch of Thoughts*, but on pluralist and secular thoughts and principles. What is more, the secular idea gained legitimacy in the political domain as well as in the cultural and literary arenas. Hence, poets and writers of the 1950s and 1960s dreamt of a Marxian revolution. While welcoming the removal of blinders and chains on eyes and hearts, they did not give up their ceaseless search for that 'Promised Dawn'. On all sides, their hopes were rekindled by Jawaharlal, the guardian of the core essence of the democratic and secular vision upheld by the framers of the Constitution, and the custodian of a multicultural inheritance.

In the 1950s and 1960s, secularism did not conflict with an individual's being, religious or otherwise. Nor did it threaten religious or caste identities. It is true that Jawaharlal faced difficulties 'creating a secular state in a religious country', but most Indians were comfortable with not just living in but extending the existing shared spaces. Historically speaking, this is where the genius of the Indian people found its most creative expression. But this picture began to change after Jawaharlal.

Spurred by nationalist feelings during the war with China (1962) and Pakistan (1965), the Jana Sangh (renamed the BJP or the Bharatiya Janata Party in 1977) increased its popular vote and share of parliamentary and assembly seats in the elections from 1952 to 1967. It sought to build a resurgent Hindu nation and revive Hindi-Hindu culture by repudiating secularism, denouncing the Congress for 'pampering Muslims' under the 'camouflage of secularism', and proposing 'Indianization' of Muslims as the ideal solution to the 'communal problem'.

Hindu parties of all hues mushroomed, and their active membership ran into several million. Besides the million RSS adherents, the urban proletariat and the unemployed youth rallied around the Vishwa Hindu Parishad. It came into being in 1964. The Hindu Manch, drawing followers from the lower middle classes, was activated after the highly publicized conversion to Islam of a few hundred Harijans in the Tamil Nadu villages of Meenakshipuram. The Hindu Shiv Sena courted the Punjabi Hindu migrants. The Ramjanmabhumi Mukti Yagya Samiti, formed in July 1984, jumped into the fray to 'liberate' the Ram temple at Ayodhya.

A set of dramatic and flamboyant demonstrations of religious worship followed. They were clearly designed to create Hindu militancy, raise the religious consciousness of Hindus and make them aware of a quite specific view of Hinduism. Thus the *Ram Shila Pujan* (bricks emblazoned with the name 'Ram' were consecrated, worshipped and aggressively paraded) was launched on 15 September 1989, followed by the *shilanyas* ceremony (the laying of the foundation stone of the

Ram temple), and, in September–October 1990, L.K. Advani's *rath yatra* from Somnath.

There are varied explanations of why Hindu nationalism became the new mantra of civil society, but what is noteworthy is that religious discontent of sorts began to simmer not because the secular state had violated any community's religious rights, but because the post-Nehruvian governments did not do enough to strengthen the secular edifice. Thus it became a routine affair to break coconuts, put vermilion on foreheads, invoke Hindu gods at state functions, and draw political mileage from religious symbols. At a time when the communal temperature was high, the government television network presented a serialization of the great Hindu epics, the Ramayana and the Mahabharata. Both fuelled the revival of religious politics.

Indira Gandhi and her refurbished party, created after the 1969 split in Congress, were fully committed to her father's secular legacy. At the same time, she possessed the skills to change course midstream, especially when her critics and adversaries mounted campaigns against the Congress. She also showed skill in accommodating the centrifugal forces to isolate and deflect the emergence of alternative political currents. For example, when she was unsure of retaining the loyalty of Muslims and the Harijans after the 1977 debacle, she developed an alternative power-base by uniting behind the upper caste Hindu vote, which on balance had been hostile to her in the past. She did not exploit, appease or compromise with Hindu communalism, a point Francin R. Frankel underlines, but she did try to preserve national unity by accommodating the claims of the minorities and the sensibilities of the Hindu majority.

Meanwhile, the Congress wooed and pandered to the religious sentiments of Muslim orthodoxy. It did so to ensure that the electoral reverses suffered by the party in by-elections were not repeated nationally. Hence the capitulation over Shah Bano, a housewife from Indore in the central Indian state of Madhya Pradesh, who approached the judicial magistrate in 1978 for a maintenance allowance of Rs 400 a month. Her husband, Ahmad Khan, for his part, said that he had divorced his wife by the irrevocable method of saying *talaq, talaq, talaq* and that he was not obliged to provide further maintenance. The magistrate ordered Ahmad Khan to pay Rs 25, later increased to Rs 179 and 20 paise. Ahmad Khan challenged the order in the Supreme Court on the plea that under the Shariat the payment of maintenance up to the end of the *iddat* period (three months following the divorce) concluded the responsibilities of the husband. India's highest court did not agree; it upheld the maintenance order under Section 125. All hell broke loose. The judgement led to bitter controversy and the mobilization of communal forces.

Rajiv Gandhi heeded the strident clamourings of the Muslim Personal Law Board (MPLB) and introduced the Muslim Women (Protection of Rights on Divorce) Act of 1986. The immediate consequences were twofold. The BJP received a fresh lease of life by using the Shah Bano episode as a powerful issue for countrywide mobilization. From 1986 onwards it dominated the ideological agenda with 'minorityism', 'pseudo-secularism', and Hindutva. In effect, therefore, the Congress abandoned its historic role of mediating between different groups in civil society and the state.

The Congress networks built over many decades weakened after Jawaharlal. The centralization of power and authority undermined party structures, weakened institutions, and created a personalized regime. As mentioned earlier, Rajiv Gandhi in 1985 had blasted the cliques that enmeshed 'the living body of the Congress in their net of avarice', and chided their 'self-aggrandizement, their corrupt ways, their linkages with vested interests and their sanctimonious posturing'. Among their many weaknesses, these cliques were not equipped to manage mounting social tensions and religious cleavage. How else does one explain a district judge disturbing the *status quo* over the Babri Masjid in Ayodhya? Why was this done? To create a Hindu constituency, or to mollify enraged feelings over the surrender on Shah Bano? B.G. Deshmukh, who joined Rajiv Gandhi as Principal Secretary in the Prime Minister's Office in 1989, believes that the Congress played the soft communalism card when it became clear that it could not outdo the BJP in getting the Hindu vote bank and at the same time was sure to lose the Muslim vote.

Arun Nehru, Rajiv Gandhi's ministerial colleague whose own conduct in the murky happenings at Ayodhya is not blameless, reported that 'in early 1986 the Muslim Women's Bill was passed to play the Muslim card; and then came the decision on Ayodhya to play the Hindu card. It was supposed to be a package deal. I knew it was a dangerous thing to do and I did not agree.'

The tacit support to the *shilanyas* ceremony in Ayodhya on 9 November 1989 was, in the opinion of *The Times of India*, 'a dangerous turning point in the history of independent India'. As if this was not enough, Rajiv Gandhi launched his election campaign in November that year from Faizabad close by, by promising to usher in *Ram Rajya* (the golden rule associated with Ram). The *sadhbhavana yatra* (march for harmony) some months after his defeat in the elections was a case of too little, too late.

Whether or not the Congress will learn from its past mistakes is hard to tell, but one clearly discerns sensitivity to the party's secular past in the pronouncements and actions of Sonia Gandhi, President of the Congress and Chairperson of the United Progressive Alliance. She realizes how pluralism and a composite way of living have kept intact the country's social and cultural fabric, how the culture of the last few centuries, as Jawaharlal relentlessly argued, has been defined by dialogue rather than combat, and how the 'crisis' of secularism is caused not by India's millions who live in peace and friendship with members of other faiths and avoid paradigms of encounter but by vested interests masquerading as guardians of faith.

To ensure that we do not inhabit a country that is at war with its own people, the Indian National Congress will be expected to mount, in unison with its partners in and outside the government, an inspired secular campaign with a strong social and economic content. It will have to redefine itself, adopt the universalistic, nay cosmopolitan, idiom of Jawaharlal Nehru, and align itself with the culture of an age, the *yuga* dharma.

'The truth is', Katherine Frank, Indira Gandhi's biographer, wrote in 2001, 'that the Gandhi cult and its political vehicle, the Congress Party, are now almost defunct. Indira Gandhi's life was measured out in funeral pyres and political resurrections, but in the twenty-first century, this cycle appears finally to have closed'. How unprophetic!

Above: Indira, as an infant. Below: Kamala Nehru with Indira. At the time of her birth, Motilal said, 'This girl is going to be worth more than a thousand grandsons'.

Facing page: Indira would often be dressed in a boy's khadi Congress volunteer uniform by her mother. Motilal gave her a *charkha* (spinning wheel) when she was just five years old.

20.5.26

Indu darling,

I was very glad to read your letter. I hope you are going to school now and also learning dancing. Betty will soon be with you. I am sorry I cannot come. Betty will bring some mangoes for you. I hope you will like them.

You should learn to speak French. But do not forget Hindi and English — otherwise your Dadu will not be able to talk with you.

Poor Chand is not quite well. She has had many styes in both her eyes and is not so fat as she was. But she is getting more and more naughty. I am going to take her to Mussoorie soon.

With love and kisses from

Your loving

Dadu

A letter from Motilal to his nine-year-old granddaughter while she was in Switzerland for her mother's treatment. Motilal chose the name Indira, a modified version of his mother's name Indrani, for her while Jawaharlal added Priyadarshini (dear to the sight).

Facing page: One of Indira Gandhi's first memories was of a bonfire at Anand Bhawan where all imported possessions were burnt—for days she was torn between the 'love of the doll...and duty towards my country'. Eventually, her sense of duty prevailed over her love for the imported doll.

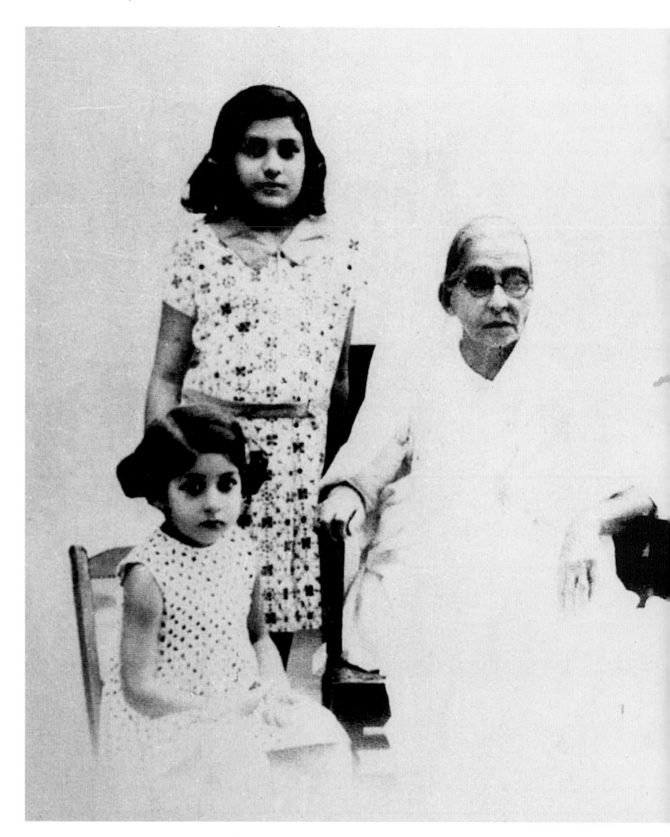

Pupul Jayakar, one of Indira Gandhi's closest friends in later life, described Kamala Nehru as the 'immovable rock in her (Indira's) life'. In a letter to her father on 29 August 1934, she wrote: 'Do you know that when Mummie was in a very bad condition the house (Anand Bhawan) was full of people, but not one of them even went to see her or sit a while with her, that when she was in agony there was no one to help her?...And with your release everything changed—people flocked from all directions, came to ask about her; sat with her.'

Left: Indira called her grandmother Swarup Rani, Dol Amma, because she gave her sweets from a *doli*, or a cabinet with doors of wire-mesh, used for storing food.

With her parents in 1931 at Anand Bhawan. The deeply religious Kamala Nehru, who had been close to Anand Mai Ma and later joined the Ramakrishna order, instilled an interest in spirituality in her daughter from a young age. Whenever Indira and her parents were together they would begin their day by reading passages from the Gita, Mahabharata or Ramayana.

Above, right and facing page: Indira was 18 years old when her mother died. In a moving letter to her, Gandhi (above right) wrote: 'Kamala's passing away had added to your responsibilities but I have no misgivings about you...Kamala possessed some qualities rarely found in other women. I am entertaining the hope that all the qualities of Kamala will be manifested in you in equal measure'. Inset: Jawaharlal's postcard to Indira.

Indira (fifth from right) studied at Santiniketan from 1934 to 1935. She had sought her father's permission to take her own cook and rent a cottage, separate from the other students. A furious Jawaharlal wrote back: 'I dislike very much the idea of your keeping apart from the "common herd" and requiring all manner of special attention, just as the Prince of Wales does when he goes to school or college. This seems to me to savour of vulgarity and snobbery.' Indira quickly adapted to the Spartan conditions at Santiniketan.

Facing page: Indira during her time at Santiniketan. Her stay at the school was cut short because of Kamala's ill-health. As Jawaharlal was in prison at the time she had to accompany her mother to Europe for medical treatment. Although her time in Santiniketan was brief, Indira was to later write to her father: 'I was glad of my stay in Santiniketan—chiefly because of Gurudev (Rabindranath Tagore)... this spirit (Tagore's) has greatly influenced my life and thought...'

40 Warwick Av
W. 9. — 3rd June 34

Dear Jawaharlalji,

Thank you so much for your letter. I hope you received the few reviews I sent you. I wonder if you would like me to send you cuttings from the 'Times' and other papers referring to you. I am enclosing one which appeared yesterday. Every few days something or other appears either about you or Bapu.

The other day London had the opportunity of seeing you in the 'News Theatre'. It was the 'Movietone News' but the editing was so bad that some one else was referred to as 'Jawahar Lal Nehru'. The film was probably shd. at a Bombay meeting.

I am going to Paris on the 15th and intend staying there for two or three months. My next exam is in the end of September.

The news from India is so disheartening that apart from getting excited I do not know what to do. I do remember word by word the conversations we have had and I am striving towards a better understanding of things in order to be of greater use than I have hitherto been.

I hope you are well. My love
From
George.

P.S. My address in Paris
60 Rue LAFAYETTE
IX. PARIS IX. 99

Facing page: Feroze Gandhi's letter to Jawaharlal written while he was in Europe. Jawaharlal and Feroze Gandhi were acquainted from the days Feroze had helped in nursing an ailing Kamala Nehru.

Indira holidaying in Kashmir. Like her father, she had a strong emotional bond with Kashmir— she was especially fascinated by the local chinar tree.

Feroze and Indira Gandhi's wedding held in Anand Bhawan on 26 March 1942. Indira Gandhi wore a light pink khadi sari which was woven from cotton yarn spun by Jawaharlal during his time in prison. Fifty-five years later, Indira Gandhi's only granddaughter Priyanka Gandhi wore the same sari on her wedding day.

The wedding of a Parsi to a Hindu created a furore amongst the orthodox Hindu community—both Jawaharlal and Gandhi had to issue statements defending the union. In his statement, Gandhi wrote: 'As time advances such unions are bound to multiply with benefit to society... The Hinduism of my conception is no narrow creed. It is a grand evolutionary process, as ancient as time and embraces the teachings of Zoroaster, Moses and other prophets I could name'.

Inset: Jawaharlal's telegram to his mother-in-law informing her of Indira's wedding date.

MRS RAJPATI KAUL
IMPERIAL BANK
NOWSHERA   (N.W.F.P.)

FIXING   INDUS   WEDDING   FOR TWENTYSIXTH   MARCH HOPE
YOU   WILL   COME   HERE   EARLY   TO   HELP   IN
ARRANGEMENTS

JAWAHARLAL

ANAND BHAWAN, ALLAHABAD   February 27, 1942

Facing page: Jawaharlal, Rajiv Gandhi and Indira Gandhi at Rajiv Gandhi's naming ceremony held on his first birthday.

When Rajiv Gandhi was born on 20 August 1944 in Bombay, Jawaharlal was in Ahmadnagar Fort Prison. When he heard the good news, G.B. Pant 'managed somehow to produce some very good and fresh *peras* at teatime to celebrate the occasion'. Before a final name was decided for the baby, he was called Rahul. However, Jawaharlal did not find it suitable because it was the name of the Buddha's son, whom the Buddha had seen as a fresh fetter attaching him

to the life he was leading and from which he wanted to get away. Twenty-six years later Indira Gandhi's first grandchild was named Rahul.

Indira Gandhi and Rajiv Gandhi at the naming ceremony which was held in Kashmir and hosted by Sheikh Abdullah. Although her husband was in Lucknow, Indira Gandhi ensured the observances of Parsi traditions at the ceremony. The final name decided was Rajiv Ratna Birjees Nehru. Jawaharlal chose Rajiv which means Lotus (as does Kamala) and Ratna which means gem (as does Jawahar).

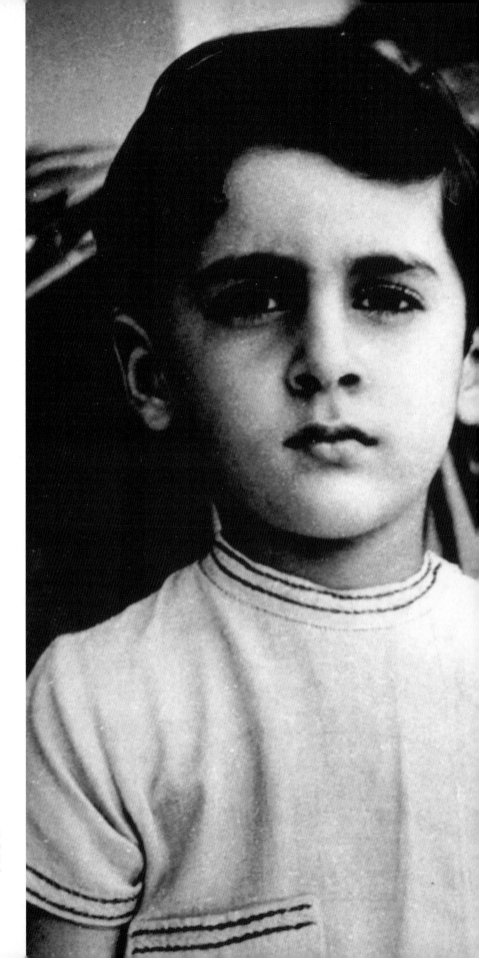

After Rajiv Gandhi (left), Indira Gandhi had been hoping for a daughter and did not have a male name ready when Sanjay Gandhi (right) was born in Delhi on 14 December 1946.

Facing page: With Sanjay Gandhi (left) and Rajiv Gandhi (right) at Palam airport, Delhi, 1949. In 1950 Indira Gandhi wrote: 'They are as different as they can be. Rajiv, the elder, is quiet and sensitive...He (Sanjay) is very talkative and lively and full of fun'.

Above, left: Rajiv Gandhi with Jawaharlal.

Above, right: Sanjay Gandhi on his father's shoulder.

Below: Rajiv Gandhi (left) and Sanjay Gandhi (right) aboard the INS Delhi, 1949.

Feroze Gandhi, Rajiv Gandhi and Vijaya Lakshmi's daughters Rita and Chandralekha (to Feroze Gandhi's left) went to see off Jawaharlal and Indira Gandhi at Palam Airport, Delhi. During this visit to the airport Rajiv Gandhi sat in the cockpit of a fighter plane for the first time.

Facing page: Indira Gandhi with Rajiv Gandhi (left) and Sanjay Gandhi (right) at Teen Murti House. Feroze Gandhi spent hours with the boys building models of planes, ships and toys—both inherited their interest in all things mechanical from him.

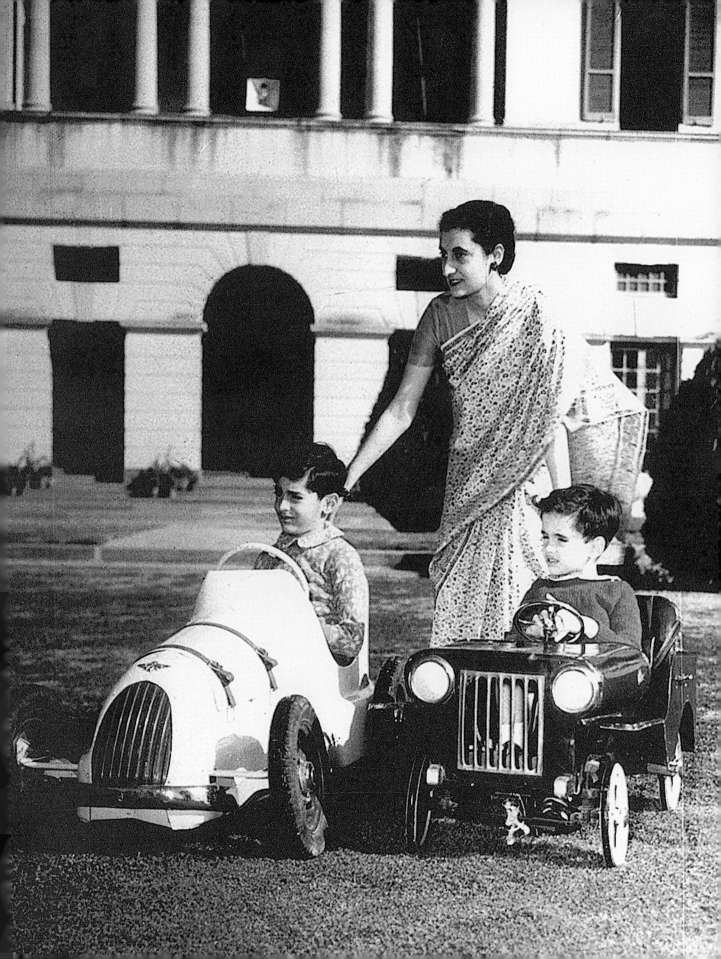

Feroze Gandhi, Sanjay Gandhi and Rajiv Gandhi (face partly hidden) at Delhi's Palam airport to bid Jawaharlal farewell before one of his foreign trips. Indira Gandhi and her two sons accompanied him to London for the Commonwealth Prime Ministers' Conference in 1955. In 1953, they had travelled to England with Jawaharlal and their mother to attend the coronation of Queen Elizabeth II.

Facing page: Jawaharlal with Sanjay Gandhi.

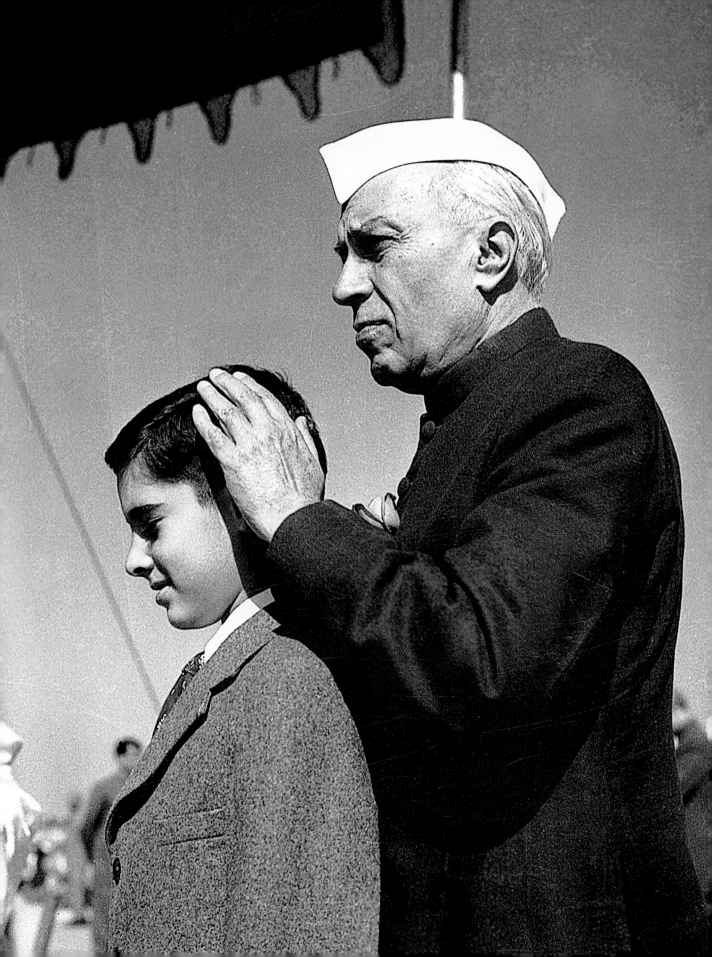

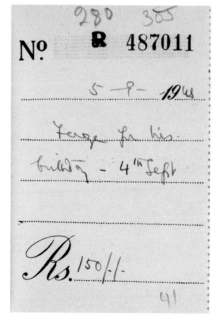

In 1946, Feroze Gandhi was appointed director of the *National Herald*, a newspaper Jawaharlal had started in 1937. While he lived in Lucknow, Indira Gandhi began to spend more time in Delhi to help her father set up home. The family lived together after the first General Elections of 1952, when Feroze Gandhi was elected to Parliament from Rae Bareilly. They lived with Jawaharlal in Teen Murti House.

Left: A birthday cheque for Feroze Gandhi from his father-in-law.

Facing page: Indira Gandhi standing in front of Anand Bhawan. Jawaharlal had left their ancestral home to her in his will. Like her grandfather had done 40 years earlier, in 1970 Indira Gandhi dedicated the house to the nation.

Facing page, top: Jawaharlal with Indira Gandhi, Rajiv Gandhi and Sanjay Gandhi, Teen Murti House. Below: Indira Gandhi with Rajiv Gandhi, Sonia Gandhi, Rahul Gandhi and Priyanka Gandhi, 1 Safdarjung Road. Sharing of meals was a family tradition which had started when Indira Gandhi and her sons lived at Teen Murti House with Jawaharlal.

Sanjay Gandhi with Feroze Gandhi whom the boys called 'Pi'. In 1958 Feroze Gandhi moved out of Teen Murti House to his bungalow at Queen Victoria Road. In the same year he suffered two heart attacks—after which the family holidayed in Kashmir together. However, the reconciliation was shortlived.

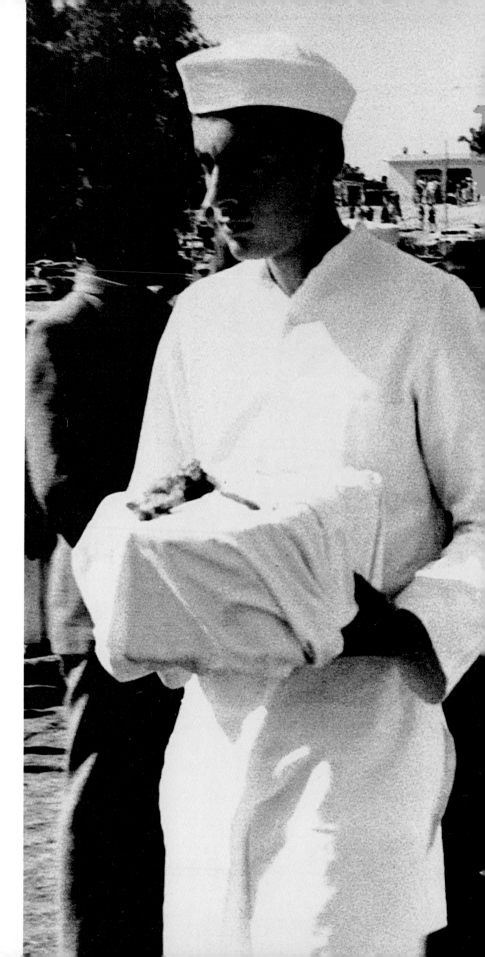

Feroze Gandhi died in Delhi on 8 September 1960. Here sixteen-year-old Rajiv Gandhi carries his father's ashes. Behind him are Indira Gandhi and Sanjay Gandhi. Although a Parsi, Feroze Gandhi wanted to be cremated because he did not like the thought of his body being exposed to the vultures in the Parsi Towers of Silence. A portion of his ashes was submerged at the Sangam and the remainder buried in the Allahabad Parsi cemetery.

Indira Gandhi in 1963. This was a year of self-reflection for her. On 8 May she wrote to her American friend Dorothy Norman: 'The question of my future is bothering me'. She even contemplated leaving India and living abroad for a few years.

Facing page: Rajiv Gandhi left for Cambridge in 1962, while Sanjay Gandhi began an apprenticeship with Rolls-Royce in England in 1964. In 1962, Indira Gandhi wrote to Dorothy Norman, 'It is rather poignant... for a mother when her child becomes a man and she knows that he is no longer dependent on her...'

Indira Gandhi continued to act as the official hostess to her father. She accompanied him on overseas trips and, as a result, witnessed politics and diplomacy first hand. Initially, she was reluctant to be an active participant in politics. In 1959, G.B. Pant is said to have convinced her to succeed the outgoing Congress President.

Jawaharlal and Indira Gandhi at a Congress meeting in 1961.

Below: With Lal Bahadur Shastri, who succeeded Jawaharlal as Prime Minister. Indira Gandhi was the Minister of Information and Broadcasting in Shastri's government. After Shastri's death in Tashkent, she became her party's choice to succeed him as Prime Minister.

Indira Gandhi's first foreign visit as Prime Minister in 1966 was to America. Her cousin, B.K Nehru (holding her hand), was India's ambassador at the time.

Below: With President Lyndon Johnson and B.K Nehru. Johnson was charmed by her and is said to have remarked that he would see that 'no harm comes to this girl' before promising three million tons of food and $9 million in aid to India.

Facing page: Indira Gandhi in Rome with Fori Nehru (extreme left) and Ambika Soni (extreme right). In 1972, during a stopover in Rome, Indira Gandhi invited a young Ambika Soni to work for the Congress Party. Soni, who was in Italy at the time as her husband worked for the Indian embassy, took up the offer. She became involved with the activities of the Youth Congress.

Facing page: Rajiv Gandhi met Sonia Maino as a student in Cambridge in 1965. They were married on 25 February 1968 at a simple civil ceremony in New Delhi. Here the newlyweds are seen with Sonia Gandhi's family and Indira Gandhi. Although Sonia Gandhi's father did not attend the wedding, many of her relatives from Italy were present, including Sonia Gandhi's mother (standing to Indira Gandhi's right), sister and maternal uncle.

Indira Gandhi was extremely fond of Sonia Gandhi, who took charge of domestic duties and her mother-in-law's personal needs. Rajiv Gandhi, by now flying the Dakota—the plane of his childhood dreams—led a simple life in the company of his family and other pilot friends.

Left: Rajiv Gandhi with Satish Sharma (also seated) during his flying years. Sharma later joined the Congress and became a Cabinet minister.

On 19 June 1970, Indira Gandhi became a grandmother following the birth of Rahul Gandhi. Here the doting grandmother shows off the baby to the Indian press soon after her electoral victory in 1971.

Feroze Gandhi with Rajiv Gandhi.
Facing page: Rajiv Gandhi with Rahul Gandhi.

The similarities between father and son went beyond their physical attributes. In a letter to her son after Feroze Gandhi's death, Indira Gandhi wrote: 'You never talk—that is, about what is really in your mind. It was this same trait in Papa which caused him so much mental suffering, and prevented me from doing so many things to help him. If you do not talk, how can I do so?'

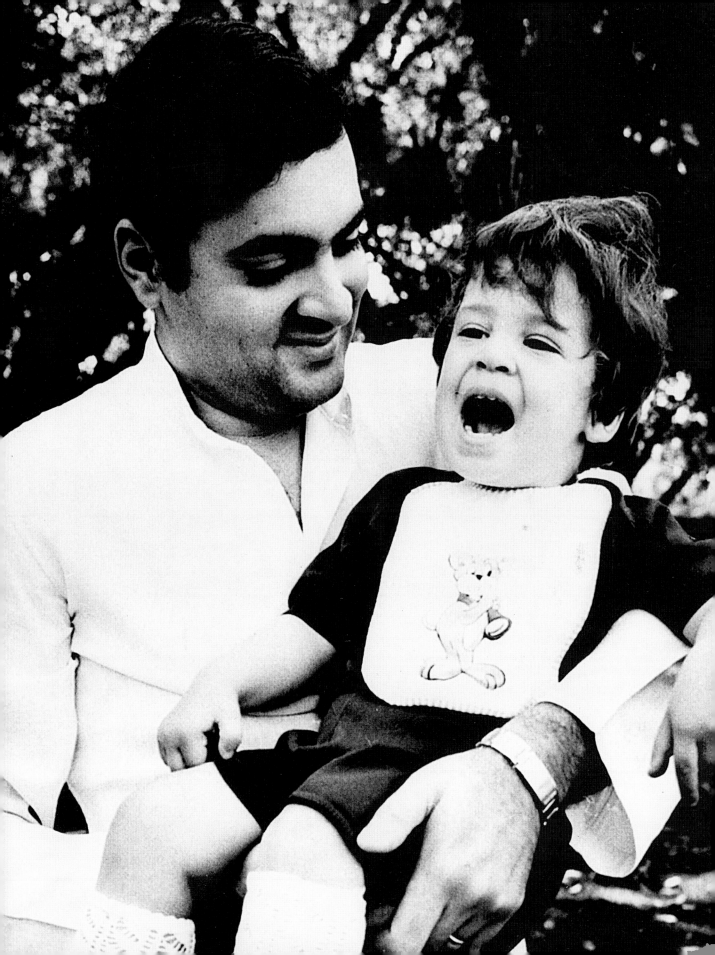

Indira Gandhi with the ascetic Acharya Vinoba Bhave, who set up an ashram in Wardha and remained a Gandhian all his life. In 1940, Gandhi had chosen him to be the first satyagrahi. In 1951 Bhave founded the Bhoodan Movement (land-gift movement) and subsequently travelled thousands of kilometres by foot, accepting donations of land for redistribution to the landless. By 1969 the movement had collected over four million acres of land for redistribution.

A rock was thrown at Indira Gandhi while she was addressing a gathering in Orissa during the 1967 election campaign. Here she is seen with President Radhakrishnan in Delhi on 10 February, two days after the incident. She had to undergo minor surgery and confessed to Fori Nehru that she had wanted something done to her nose (a lifelong desire) but the doctors treating her were not trained in plastic surgery.

Right: Indira Gandhi during an election campaign.

Clockwise from top: Rajiv Gandhi, Rahul Gandhi, Sonia Gandhi and Priyanka Gandhi, born on 11 January 1971. Her birth coincided with the creation of Bangladesh—a great political victory for Indira Gandhi; Indira Gandhi fixing Priyanka Gandhi's button; Rahul Gandhi and Priyanka Gandhi. Before 1980 Rajiv Gandhi's world was very different from that of his mother and brother's. He kept a distance from politics and chose to clock air miles as a pilot, dabble in photography and spend time with his family.
Facing page: Indira Gandhi and Priyanka Gandhi.

Talking to soldiers in a forward area in Punjab, 1971. The victory over the Pakistani forces and the subsequent founding of Bangladesh elevated Indira Gandhi's political and popular standing.

Below: In March 1972, Indira Gandhi visited Bangladesh. She signed a treaty of friendship, cooperation and peace with Mujibur Rahman, the founding leader of Bangladesh.

After India's victory in the 1971 war with Pakistan, Indira Gandhi was elevated to a goddess-like status—newborn girls were named after her and she was increasingly referred to as Mother India.

Above and facing page: Unlike Rajiv Gandhi, Sanjay Gandhi showed a keen interest in politics. In 1971 Indira Gandhi's Cabinet granted him the prized license to produce the people's car—Maruti. This led to fierce criticism.

Facing page: Sanjay Gandhi, Rajiv Gandhi, Sonia Gandhi and Indira Gandhi, New Delhi, December 1968.

Top: Sanjay and Maneka Gandhi were married on 29 September 1974 in a civil ceremony at the home of family friend Mohammed Yunus. Sanjay Gandhi and Menaka had met for the first time at Yunus' home the previous December. Indira Gandhi gave Maneka her mother's engagement ring, which had been designed by Motilal. From Left: Rajiv Gandhi, Indira Gandhi, Maneka's parents Colonel T. S Anand and Amteshwar Anand, brother Virendra and sister Ambika; Seated: Sanjay Gandhi, family friend Naveen Chawla, Maneka and Mohammad Yunus.

Above, left: The invitation card for their wedding reception. Maneka was 17 and Sanjay Gandhi 28 when they wed.

Above, right: Rajiv Gandhi feeds guests at his brother's wedding.

Above and right: When Sanjay Gandhi was killed in a flying accident on June 23 1980, Indira Gandhi was emotionally shattered. To comprehend the tragedy she visited the crash site twice. Yet, she returned to work just four days after her younger son's ashes were submerged in Allahabad. But this was a different Indira Gandhi: in the aftermath of Sanjay Gandhi's death she became politically insecure. She now turned to Rajiv Gandhi to help her shoulder the political responsibilities.

After Sanjay Gandhi's death, Menaka Gandhi's relations soured with the Gandhi family. She left her mother-in-law's home in the middle of the night on 29 March 1982.

Facing page: Sanjay Gandhi and Maneka Gandhi's son, Feroze Varun, with Indira Gandhi and Rajiv Gandhi's family. Feroze Varun was three months old when his father died.

Indira Gandhi was known for immense energy during election campaigns. In the run-up to the 1980 elections she was especially charged—spending 62 days on the road, covering 40,000 miles and addressing up to twenty meetings a day. The Congress won 351 out of 542 Lok Sabha seats and Indira Gandhi was sworn in as Prime Minister for the fourth time on 14 January 1980.

"Poverty must be eradicated...
Disparities between the rich and
poor should be reduced... The
backward people, be they harijans,
adivasis or the hill people should
have equal opportunities to make
progress and there should be an
equal distribution of national
income.

This is our socialism
This is our goal

Indira Gandhi

by ERIC FRANCIS —

MUNSHI MUBARAK ALI, THE OLD MAN WHO MANAGED THE AFFAIRS OF THE HOUSE-HOLD OF ANAND BHAWAN, THE HOME OF MOTILAL NEHRU, LAY DYING OF CANCER. ONE DAY HE SPOKE TO MOTILAL...

BHAI SAHIB, I CANNOT DIE TILL I HAVE HELD JAWAHARLAL'S CHILD IN MY ARMS AND BLESSED IT

AND SO IT WAS. SOON AFTER KAMALA NEHRU DELIVERED HER BABY, THE CHILD WAS TAKEN TO THE AILING MUNSHIJI. INDIRA WAS BORN ON 19TH NOVEMBER 1917. TEARS OF JOY TRICKLED DOWN, AS HE TOOK THE CHILD IN HIS ARMS...

MAY THIS LITTLE ONE ENJOY ALLAH'S CHOICEST BLESSINGS AND PROVE A WORTHY HEIR TO JAWAHAR

THEN HE WENT ON...

MOTILAL'S "GRANDSON" WILL BY THE GRACE OF GOD, ILLUMINATE THE NAME OF THE NEHRUS

I did not skx skip school but political talk was not
limited to certain time. It was taking place all over
the house, all the time – day and night. Romain Rolland
should say I admire your struggle and non-violent method.

Page -8

In Switzerland I went first to International School run
by League of Nations and later to another in the mountains.
The family travelled in other parts of Europe also.

(This picture is wrong)

The whole family returned together to the humming activity
of Anand Bhavan. In fact/life in Europe was quieter and
even lonlier than in Allahabad. In Lahore my father
made out the Resolution on complete Independence and
said that now you also are committed to it.

Page -9 (Pledge should go to page -8)

Page -10 We had all come back together

(This is wrong)

I went to a school run by a Cambridge friend of JN, Mr. Vakil.

Nobody should be wearing dresses.

There was no mock Parliament.

This comic book (this page and following pages 298–299), created by Eric Francis, was not published because of Indira Gandhi's assassination. However, she had taken great interest in the project—often commenting on the quality of the sketches ('bad picture' on first picture), correcting facts and omitting certain events.

...AND MOBILISED THE PEOPLE FOR THE DEFENCE OF THE COUNTRY...

OUR JAWANS ARE GIVING THEIR LIVES FOR THE NATION. WE MUST DO EVERYTHING TO MAKE THEM FEEL THAT WE ARE WHOLE-HEARTEDLY BEHIND THEM

TEN DAYS LATER A CEASEFIRE WAS ANNOUNCED AND THE CHINESE FORCES WITHDREW.

BUT THE SPIRIT OF NEHRU REMAINED DEEPLY WOUNDED

AT THE BHUBANESHWAR SESSION OF THE INDIAN NATIONAL CONGRESS, HE SUFFERED A HEART ATTACK IN JANUARY 1964

GOOD HEAVENS! PANDITJI HAS GOT A HEART ATTACK

INDIRA SPENT FOUR MONTHS NURSING HER AILING FATHER

PAPU, COME, GET UP AND HAVE THIS GLASS OF FRUIT JUICE

ON THE NIGHT OF 26TH MAY 1961 HE CLEARED ALL HIS ARREARS OF WORK...

GOOD. EVERYTHING IS DONE. I THINK I WILL NOW GO TO BED.

IN THE MORNING HE COLLAPSED WITH A STROKE AND NEVER RECOVERED CONSCIOUSNESS.

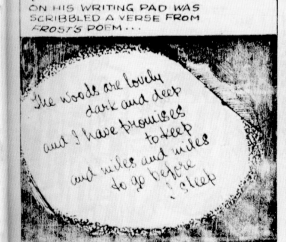

ON HIS WRITING PAD WAS SCRIBBLED A VERSE FROM FROST'S POEM...

The woods are lovely dark and deep and I have promises to keep and miles and miles to go before I sleep

FOR HOURS INDIRA SAT AT HIS BEDSIDE TILL HE PASSED AWAY ON 27TH MAY 1964

THE WAR WAS ON. ON 4TH DECEMBER 1971 MRS. GANDHI'S BROADCAST WAS HEARD WITH DEEP ATTENTION

I SPEAK TO YOU AT A MOMENT OF GREAT PERIL TO OUR COUNTRY AND OUR PEOPLE.
PAKISTAN HAS LAUNCHED A FULL SCALE WAR AGAINST INDIA.
TODAY THE WAR IN BANGLA DESH HAS BECOME A WAR ON INDIA.
AGGRESSION MUST BE MET AND THE PEOPLE OF INDIA WILL MEET IT WITH FORTITUDE, DETERMINATION, DISCIPLINE AND UTMOST UNITY.

AS WAS EXPECTED, ALL POLITICAL PARTIES SUNK THEIR DIFFERENCES AND SUPPORTED THE PRIME MINISTER.

MADAM, WE ARE ALL WITH YOU, IRRESPECTIVE OF OUR IDEOLOGIES

WITH THE INDIAN ARMED FORCES GOING INTO ACTION BANGLA DESH WAS ATTACKED FROM ALL SIDES

ON 16TH DECEMBER 1971 MRS. GANDHI ANNOUNCED IN PARLIAMENT...

THE PAKISTAN FORCES IN BANGLA DESH HAVE SURRENDERED UNCONDITIONALLY IN DACCA AT 16·31 HOURS

THIS WAS FOLLOWED BY A FURTHER ANNOUNCEMENT.

THE UNILATERAL CEASE FIRE ON THE WESTERN FRONT HAS BEEN ACCEPTED WITH EFFECT FROM 20 HOURS ON THE 17TH DECEMBER.

THE WAR WAS OVER. IN TOKEN OF HER GREAT SERVICE TO INDIA, THE PRESIDENT CONFERRED ON HER INDIA'S HIGHEST AWARD – THE BHARAT RATNA.

THE BHARAT RATNA, INDIA'S HIGHEST AWARD IS HEREBY CONFERRED ON MRS. GANDHI...

IN THE 1972 STATE ELECTIONS, INDIRA GANDHI AND HER PARTY SWEPT THE POLLS.

THE OPPOSITION WANT "INDIRA HATAO" BUT WHAT I WANT IS "GARIBI HATAO".

ON 27TH MAY 1972, A "NEHRU CAPSULE CONTAINING A CHRONICLE OF THE NEHRU ERA WAS BURIED AT SHANTIVANA IN DELHI.

Indira Gandhi and Fidel Castro with leaders of other non-aligned nations at the Seventh Non-Aligned Summit held in New Delhi on March 7 1983. Indira Gandhi presided over the summit.

Indira Gandhi with Ronald Reagan at the White House in 1982. Rajiv Gandhi (standing left, next to Nancy Reagan) accompanied his mother. During this press conference, a reporter asked Indira Gandhi why India always titled towards the Soviet Union. Her reply: 'We do not tilt on either side... we walk upright'.

Facing page: In January 1981 Rajiv Gandhi had qualified to fly Boeings—an exciting landmark in a pilot's career. However, due to mounting pressure, four months later he resigned from the airline to contest the Amethi byelections.

Facing page: Indira Gandhi being presented with a picture of Guru Nanak by traditional Punjabi dancers. The Sikhs did not forgive the Prime Minister for desecrating their holiest shrine, the Golden Temple, in Amritsar during Operation Blue Star.

Indira Gandhi visited the Golden Temple on June 25 1984, weeks after Operation Blue Star. In the aftermath of the army operation, she knew that her life was in danger. Just one night before her assassination, she had said: 'I shall continue to serve until my last breath and when I die, I can say that every drop of my blood will invigorate India and strengthen it'.

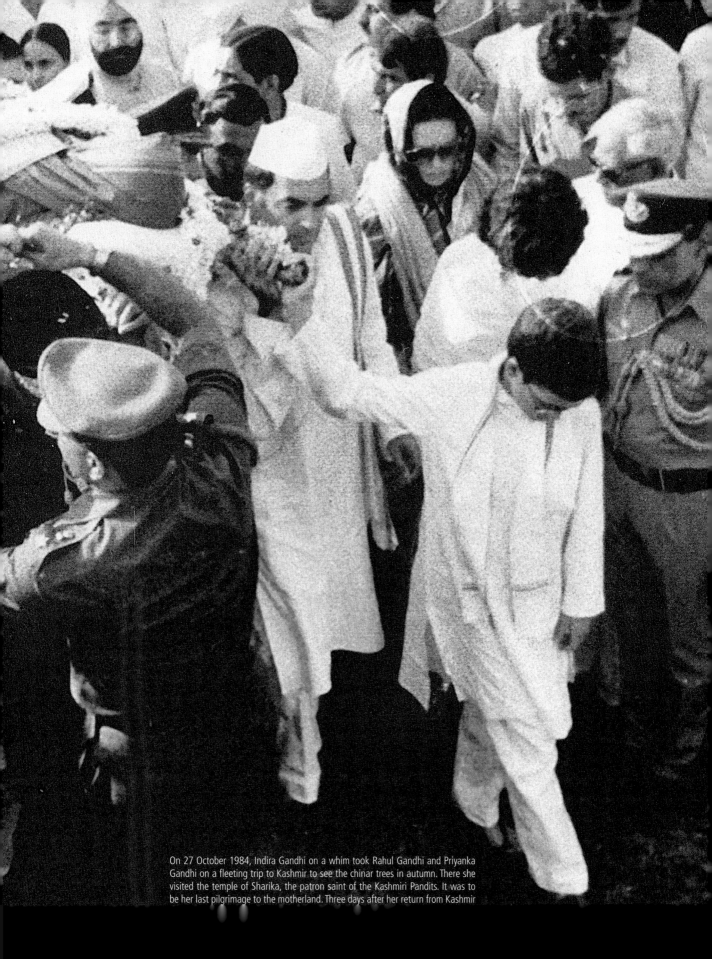

On 27 October 1984, Indira Gandhi on a whim took Rahul Gandhi and Priyanka Gandhi on a fleeting trip to Kashmir to see the chinar trees in autumn. There she visited the temple of Sharika, the patron saint of the Kashmiri Pandits. It was to be her last pilgrimage to the motherland. Three days after her return from Kashmir

Facing page: Rajiv Gandhi with Ronald Reagan at the White House in 1987. During an earlier visit to the United States in 1985, he had addressed the American Congress in the following words: 'India is an old country but a young nation... I am young, and I too have a dream. I dream of an India—strong, independent, self-reliant and in the front rank of the nations of the world in the service of mankind...'

The sixth Prime Minister of India, Rajiv Gandhi, with members of the Council of Ministers after the swearing in ceremony on 31 December 1984. Rajiv Gandhi was sworn in as Prime Minister the same evening as Indira Gandhi's assassination took place. However, elections were held in November 1984. The Congress received the highest ever mandate in an Indian election. Rajiv Gandhi, at 40, became India's youngest Prime Minister.

Rajiv Gandhi with the Soviet leader Leonid Brezhnev. High up on Rajiv Gandhi's agenda was the advancement of science and technology in India in order to prepare the country for the 21st century.

Rajiv Gandhi receiving Palestinian leader Yasser Arafat, when the latter called on him in New Delhi in 1985. Arafat shared a good relationship with both Indira Gandhi and Rajiv Gandhi—he referred to Indira Gandhi as 'my sister'.

In 1986, Rajiv Gandhi and Soviet President Mikhail Gorbachev signed the Delhi Declaration, which proposed a New World Order, characterized by non-violence and principles of peaceful coexistence.

Rajiv Gandhi with Ziaul Haq during the Pakistani leader's visit to New Delhi in 1985. In 1988, Rajiv Gandhi became the first Indian Prime Minister since Jawaharlal to visit Pakistan. Rajiv Gandhi went to Pakistan to attend a SAARC summit.

On 21 May 1991, Rajiv Gandhi was assassinated by a suicide bomber while campaigning in Tamil Nadu. He lay in state for two days at Teen Murti House, where his grandfather and mother had also rested before their cremation.

Below: Rahul Gandhi, Sonia Gandhi, Priyanka Gandhi and Amitabh Bachchan inside the special train carrying Rajiv Gandhi's ashes to Allahabad, 27 May 1991. The next day, following the family tradition, his ashes were immersed in the Sangam.

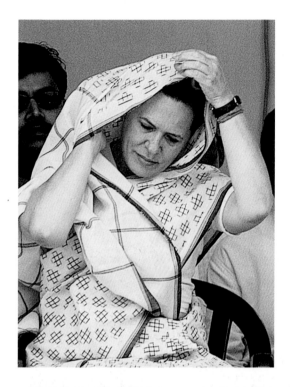

Top left and right: After Rajiv Gandhi's death there was immense pressure for Sonia Gandhi to join politics. However she declined to do so until 1998. Her campaigning style is said to resemble that of Indira Gandhi's.

Below: Prime Minister Dr. Manmohan Singh being greeted by Rehaan, son of Priyanka and Robert Vadra, at the Vir Bhoomi on the occasion of Rajiv Gandhi's 60th birth anniversary in New Delhi, 2004. Also seen are Sonia Gandhi and Rahul Gandhi.

Facing page: Besides her personal charisma, Indira Gandhi's approach and simple style drew huge crowds. Her stamina and energy during elections led her to travel thousands of miles across the country in just a few days.

Soon after leading the Congress party to victory in the 2004 general elections, Sonia Gandhi declined the Prime Minister's post, choosing instead to remain as Congress President and assume the role of United Progressive Alliance Chairperson.

Facing page: Rahul Gandhi with sister Priyanka Gandhi Vadra and her husband Robert Vadra. In 2004, Rahul Gandhi was elected MP from Amethi, the seat of power of the Nehru-Gandhi family. He became the fourth in his family to win the seat from this constituency.

© Roli & Janssen BV 2006
This edition published in 2006 by
Mercury Books
20 Bloomsbury Street
London, WCIB 3JH
in arrangement with
Roli & Janssen BV
The Netherlands

ISBN: 1-84560-019-3

Editor: Priya Kapoor, Amit Agarwal
Design: Sneha Pamneja
Layout: Naresh Mondal

Printed and bound in Singapore